CW01085251

RAF IN GALLOWAY

by

A. T. Murchie

"And make the great grey roaring thing
Turn out, and leap and take to wing:
Then, watching still her twinkling light,
They see her disappear from sight:-
Then after her their wishes yearn:-
"O beautiful great bird, return.
Sweep home to-morrow from the blue,
And bring our kinsman home with you."

John Masefield
"Ground Staff" 1942

ISBN 1 872350 18 6

G.C. Book Publishers Ltd
Wigtown
Scotland DG8 9HL
Tel/Fax: 01988 40 2499
gcbooks@demon.co.uk
Printed by MPG Books Ltd
Bodmin, Cornwall

CONTENTS

List of Illustrations

Foreword

Preface   6

1. Aircraft from RAF Training Command on a routine stop at West Freugh on 6th January 1999.

List of Illustrations

THE ROYAL AIR FORCE
IN GALLOWAY

PREFACE

On 1 April 1918 the Royal Flying Corps merged with the Royal Naval Air Service to form the Royal Air Force. Before this date the Royal Flying Corps visited Wigtownshire in 1913 and the Royal Naval Air Service commenced flying airships from a Wigtownshire base in June 1915. To give a full record of military flying in Galloway, the RFC visit in 1913 as recorded in contemporary issues of the '*Wigtown Free Press* ' and the '*Galloway Gazette* ', and the RNAS activities from 1915 to 1918 are included herein.

Notes on the various Units and their varied roles from 1914 to 1959 are based on the original Station, Squadron and other Unit records held in the Public Record Office.

Records of West Freugh in the period between 1960 and 1999 are in the main based on Ministry of Defence Press Release notices together with advice on present practice given by the Test and Evaluation Establishment at West Freugh.

Thanks are due to the Public Record Office and to others who helped by loaning documents, permitting use of photographs etc, and to the many 'ex RAF bods' who have written since the first edition of this book was published in 1992, pointing out errors and omissions and giving additional information.

CHAPTER 1

2 SQUADRON, ROYAL FLYING CORPS

The first aeroplane to land in Galloway was a French built Maurice Farman MF7 single engine biplane with a pusher airscrew which landed at Cults Farm, Castle Kennedy on 10 August 1913. This plane was from 2 Squadron, Royal Flying Corps which had been based at Panmure Barracks, Montrose, since February 1913. During the following seven days, five British built BE2 planes from 2 Squadron arrived at Cults, those which flew direct from Montrose making the journey in two hours fifteen minutes. Prior permission to land at Cults had been obtained from the owner of the land, the Earl of Stair.

The BE2 was designed by Geoffrey de Havilland who was then employed by the Royal Aircraft Factory at Farnborough, Hampshire. This single engine biplane was the first British military aircraft to be produced in quantity. During World War I the BE2 series ranging from BE2a to BE2f was produced by twenty-two different manufacturers who built more than 3,500. It had a maximum speed of 72 mph and a ceiling of 6,500 feet.

All six planes were en route to Rathbone Camp in County Limerick to take part in Army manoeuvres. During their stay at Cults, the planes had flotation bags fitted to their undercarriages prior to making the "lengthy sea crossing" between Portpatrick and Newcastle, County Down where they were to land on the beach. Five departed for Ireland on 27 August, the final BE2 leaving on 2 September having waited for replacement of a damaged propeller. Sections of this damaged propeller are held by the Wigtown District Museum, Stranraer.

After completion of the Army exercise, four planes set off on the return journey to Cults leaving behind one BE2 and the

Maurice Farman which were unserviceable. One BE2 flying direct arrived safely at Cults on 25 September followed by another which arrived on 26 September after an overnight stop at Newcastle. The third also flying from Newcastle landed near Troon in Ayrshire having become completely lost. The final BE2 overflew Cults in poor visibility to land at Holm Park close to Minnigaff, Newton Stewart. Having ascertained his location, the pilot took off to follow the railway line to Castle Kennedy but in error followed the Wigtown line. Realising his error he returned to land again at Holm Park to obtain fuel before finally reaching Cults. Later that afternoon the three remaining aircraft departed for Montrose.

These visiting aircraft created tremendous local interest. Roads leading to Castle Kennedy were reported to be crowded with charabancs, horse carriages, bicycles and other conveyances carrying all and sundry to see the aeroplanes. The Portpatrick and Wigtownshire Railway Company ran an excursion train from Whithorn to Castle Kennedy on Saturday 30 August calling at all eight intermediate stations. Return fare from Whithorn was 2/9d (14p). On 26 September lessons were suspended at Kirkcowan school when it was learned that an aeroplane would pass overhead following the railway line from Newton Stewart to Castle Kennedy. Earlier that day Newton Stewart schools had been closed for two hours to allow pupils to visit Holm Park.

The Galloway Creamery in Stranraer which habitually advertised their own brand of butter in the 'Wigtown Free Press' regretted in their advertisement on 28 August that "your grocer cannot yet deliver our cream butter by aeroplane".

Less than one year later 2 Squadron was the first Royal Flying Corps unit to arrive in France after the outbreak of World War I. Flying BE2 and other aircraft they remained in France until 1918 during which time two of the Squadron pilots were awarded the Victoria Cross.

2. BE2 No 273, 2 Squadron, Royal Flying Corps, Cults Farm. August 1913

3. BE2 No 225, 2 Squadron, Royal Flying Corps, Holm Park, Newton Stewart. 26th September, 1913

4. Maurice Farman MF7 No. 207, 2 Squadron, Royal Flying Corps, Cults Farm. August, 1913

CHAPTER 2

ROYAL NAVAL AIR STATION - LUCE BAY

Almost two years now elapsed before the requirements of World War I brought further aviation to Galloway. Concerned by increasing U-Boat activity, the Admiralty decided to establish Airship Stations to provide anti-submarine patrols over the Irish Sea and North Channel. Thus in June 1915 Royal Naval Air Station, Luce Bay opened at East Freugh five miles south east of Stranraer. By early August two Sea Scout Airships, SS17 and SS23 had arrived followed shortly by SS33. These were non-rigid airships 146 feet in length with a hydrogen gas capacity of 70,000 cubic feet. The engine and crew of two were housed in an open cockpit aircraft fuselage slung underneath the balloon. The fuselages used were either Maurice Farman or BE2. Normal operational endurance was up to sixteen hours. The first operational patrol was undertaken on 23 August. During the next two years in addition to many short duration training flights, regular anti-submarine and convoy escort patrols were carried out by SS airships together with the important task of escorting SS *Princess Maud* on her daily sailings on the Stranraer to Larne ferry service.

In mid-1917 the Sea Scout Zero, a new airship with a crew of three which had a cruising speed of thirty knots, came into service: SSZ11, SSZ12 and SSZ13 arrived at Luce Bay in July 1917 followed in October by SSZ20. Each SSZ airship was said to cost £2,500.

On 20 August 1917, SSZ11 returning from a patrol to the south suffered a complete engine failure. At the mercy of strong south westerly winds the pilot managed to make a landing on high ground between Larg Hill and Bennan Hill seven miles north east of Newton Stewart and twenty-four miles from East Freugh. Fortunately the crew were uninjured and little damage was sustained by the airship which was later stripped down on site to be sent by rail to London for repair. Just over one year later SSZ13 was completely wrecked on 30 August 1918 when, following an engine failure, a forced landing was made in the sea at Castlehead Point near Rockcliffe. The crew of three were uninjured.

In 1918 SSZ12 was airborne for 984 hours flying 23,560 miles whilst SSZ20 was airborne for 1,263 hours flying 28,290 miles. During a little over three years of wartime operation, airships from Luce Bay flew many thousands of miles on patrol and escort duties during which attacks were made on suspected submarine locations but no hits were recorded. In a paper written after the war for the RAF Staff College, a former Luce Bay pilot explained that the role of the airship was generally a passive one. By denying the submarine the ability to surface freely, long periods of submersion created considerable discomfort for the crew. When surfaced submarines could usually sight an airship before being themselves sighted allowing time to submerge; however if the submarine was revealed the airship could contact the anti-submarine surface vessels which patrolled the Irish Sea and North Channel. German sources conceded that airship patrols had a strong deterrent effect.

With the formation of the Royal Air Force on 1 April 1918, Luce Bay became the first RAF Station in Galloway. In July 1918 two Flights from 255 Squadron each with four De Havilland DH6 single engine biplanes were sent to Luce Bay to provide inshore patrol cover for North Channel shipping. Shortly afterward when a third Flight arrived, 258 Squadron was formed equipped with twelve DH6s. The first 258 Squadron patrols were flown on 7 August when seven DH6s patrolled the coastline between Mull of Galloway and Ballantrae.

In retrospect it can be seen that the DH6 did not pose much risk to a U-Boat. After a short period of operational use in France it had been relegated to a training role in which capacity it was soon replaced by the Avro 504k. Only then were a number allocated to 255 and 258 Squadrons. Top speed of 70 mph with an endurance of two-and-a-half hours meant that range was limited and armament of one twenty pound bomb would not do much damage. However as with the airships they had a deterrent effect. Weather and other conditions permitting patrols of the coastal area bounded roughly by Burrowhead, Mull of Galloway and Ballantrae continued until the end of war on 11 November 1918. With no further active role 258 Squadron was disbanded in December 1918.

5. Sea Scout Airship SS38, Royal Naval Air Station, East Freugh. September, 1916

RAFM P1042

6. Sea Scout Airship preparing for take off, Royal Naval Air Station, East Freugh. June 1917   D. Nelson

7. De Havilland DH6 258 Squadron, East Freugh. August, 1918   IWMQ68131

CHAPTER 3

ROYAL AIR FORCE STATION WEST FREUGH

Other than flying boat activities in Loch Ryan which are recorded elsewhere, the RAF did not return to Galloway until August 1936 when the Air Ministry purchased 2,700 acres of land at West Freugh at a cost of £19,400. Later wartime expansion absorbed East Freugh, site of the former Airship Station.

On 1 January 1937 4 Armament Training Camp, West Freugh, housing 4 Bombing and Gunnery School, was formally opened. From this date until April 1939 a large number of squadrons visited the station for periods of from four to six weeks to undertake bombing and gunnery training. During this time the list of visiting aircraft types included Battle, Blenheim, Demon, Harrow, Hart, Hector, Heyford, Hind, Overstrand, Wellesley and Whitley. Training facilities were also provided for flying boat squadrons flying London, Singapore and Stranraer aircraft from Loch Ryan. The airfield had two concrete runways, one 1,500 yards by 50 yards and one 965 yards by 50 yards. Initially there were seven Bellman hangars; later during the war years eight Blister hangars were added.

4 Bombing and Gunnery School soon after formation sought approval for a Unit Crest of the style then in use by many RAF units. These crests, following Naval and Army practice, are designed in Heraldic style and require the approval of the Inspector of RAF Badges, who is an Officer of the College of Arms. Approval was duly obtained early in 1938.

Badges are required to be circular in form with a frame of laurel within which appears the Unit title and a distinctive emblem. The badge is 'ensigned' with a Royal crown and has a motto in a scroll beneath.

In heraldic terms, the emblem of 4 Bombing and Gunnery School consists of 'An erect spider in a triangle' with the single word motto, 'Perseverance'. Taken in conjunction, emblem and motto clearly refer to Robert the Bruce, King of Scots, who has many connections with Galloway. In spring 1307, Bruce was hiding in the Carrick Hills whilst conducting guerrilla warfare against the armies of King Edward I of England. Legend has it that when he learned that Edward had hanged his three brothers, imprisoned his wife and daughter together with his sisters, he was overcome by grief. He retired to a cave where he saw a spider swinging the thread on which it was hanging in an endeavour to reach the wall of the cave. Six attempts failed before a seventh succeedeed. Bruce thereupon vowed that if a tiny insect could persevere to success then the King of Scots could do no less.

When the unit name changed in April 1939 to 4 Air Observer School., the badge was retained with tthe appropriate name change.

On 28 May 1938 the Station was opened to the general public for an Empire Air Day flying display. Anson, Battle, Heyford and Wallace aircraft all displayed their flying skills as did London and Singapore flying boats from 201 and 209 Squadrons flying from Loch Ryan.

Squadron records of 218 Squadron based at Upper Heyford show that eight Hawker Hinds visited 4 Armament Training Camp from 24 April 1937 until 24 May 1937 when training included "box formation bombing". On 12 May 1937 the Squadron participated in a parade to commemorate the Coronation that day of King George VI. Now based at Boscome Down the Squadron returned to 4 ATC from 1 June to 30 June 1938 for armament training with their newly acquired Fairey Battles. On 2 September 1939 they were amongst the first RAF Squadrons to go to action stations when they flew with sixteen Battles to Auberieve in Northern France.

A typical squadron report of this period is that of 63 (Bomber) Squadron based at Upwood, Hampshire which visited West Freugh from 30 August to 23 September 1938 with the full Squadron complement of thirteen Fairey Battles with which they had been equipped in July 1937. Their training schedule specified high and low level bombing, dive bombing, air to air and air to ground gunnery. In 390 flying hours 1,150 eleven pound practice bombs were dropped and 29,000 .303 rounds were fired.

105 Squadron flew eleven Battles in formation from their base at Harwell to West Freugh on 30 January 1939. The following day Battle K9340 suffered an engine failure over Luce Bay. Not having sufficient height to reach the airfield to land, the pilot managed to make a wheels-up forced landing on the beach at Sandhead. The crew of three were uninjured but the aircraft "could not be salved before being immersed by the rising tide and had to be written off". On 2 February the '*Wigtown Free Press*' reported under the headline "Machine's Forced Descent Causes Alarm" that an RAF machine had made a forced descent, losing height rapidly to land in a cloud of spray and after whirling around finally came to rest among (sic) the wet sand.

On 17 April 1939 the Unit accepted a wider training role when it became 4 Air Observer School. This School was equipped with 1930 vintage Handley Page Heyfords to train Observers in navigation, bombing and gunnery.

The Heyford was an ungainly twin engined biplane with a fixed undercarriage. Two 575 hp Rolls Royce Kestrel engines gave a maximum speed of 140 mph. A crew of four was carried.

On 26 February 1935 a Heyford was used in one of the first practical demonstrations of radar techniques when Robert Watson-Watt using a BBC short-wave transmitter at Daventry obtained a response on a cathode ray tube from a Heyford flying several miles away.

When war was declared on 3 September 1939 the aircraft strength of the School was twenty-one Handley Page Heyfords, twenty-one Hawker Henleys, eighteen Westland Wallaces, four Fairey Battles and two Miles Magisters. Some aircraft continued to be detached from other units for bombing and gunnery training; for example Hart, Audax, Oxford and Fury planes were detached from the Flying School attached to the Royal Air Force College at Cranwell, Lincolnshire, for four week periods in October 1939 and again in December 1939. Fleet Air Arm aircraft also visited for gunnery and bombing training; in March 1940 twelve Fairey Swordfishes visited for three weeks and in February 1941 Grumman Martlets and Blackburn Skuas from Royal Naval Air Station, Donibristle stayed for three weeks.

When on 15th October 1939, a former trainee of 4 Bombing and Gunnery School was awarded a Distinguished Flying Medal, the Commanding Officer decided that the school should thereafter maintain a formal record of all such awards. A 'Roll of Achievement' board was installed on which the name of this first recipient and each future recipient was to be recorded. As time passed, this became a lengthy task for the Orderly Room clerks detailed to check each issue of the 'London Gazette' to identify awards made to an ever-growing list of former trainees. Each name, with the name and date of the award, was carved on a strip of hardwood, then gilded before being mounted on a finely made hardwood board, headed with the unit crest and name, which had space for eighty recipients names. The last name entered records a Distinguished Flying Medal, awarded on 21st November 1941. This board, carefully maintained, is still held in the former Sergeants Mess at West Freugh. If further boards were erected, then they have not survived. The eighty awards recorded comprise 67 Distinguished Flying Medals; 11 Distinguished Flying Crosses; one Croix de Guerre and one Victoria Cross. It is invidious to select one name from amongst this list of gallant men. However, an exception can be made in respect of Sergeant John Hannah, who was awarded the Victoria Cross on 1st October 1940.

John Hannah, born in Paisley on 27th November 1921, joined the RAF on a six year engagement on 15th August 1939. After training he qualified as a Wireless Operator in March 1940. At this point he volunteered for flying duties hence his next posting was to West Freugh, where in April 1940 he was amongst the last trainees to complete an Air Gunnery Course flying in Fairey Battles. Further trtaining followed at Upper Heyford where he qualified as a Sergeant Wireless Operator/Air Gunner on 27th May 1940.

On 11th August 1940, he joined 83 Squadron based at

Scampton, Lincolnshire to fly operationally in Handley Page Hampden Bombers. On 15th September he was wireless operator in the four man crew of Hampden P1335 which took off with fourteen others to bomb German invasion barges assembling in Antwerp docks.

Flying at 2000 feet severe flak was encountered over the target. With the rear fuselage engulfed in flames the air gunner was forced to bail out. As the intercom was out of action, the pilot asked the navigator to check on the others but as he was unable to make any contact he told the pilot that the other crew members had apparently been killed or had bailed out. He was told that he should bail out and the pilot would follow him.

Meantime, though severely burned, Hannah had used two fire extinguishers before tackling the flames with his Wireless Operator's log, then with his bare hands.With the flames receding, he managed to reach the pilot who was about to abandon the aircraft. As Hannah had lost his parachute in the flames they decided to 'go home'. Showing considerable fortitude, they did just that, landing at Scampton at 3 am on 16th September. Hannah was rushed to hospital where he remained until 7th October. On 10th October, he attended an investiture at Buckingham Palace to receive the Victoria Cross, an award which had been promulgated on 1st October, together with the award of a Distinguished Flying Cross to his pilot.

Hannah did not return to operational flying, becoming instead a Signals instructor. Despite thorough medical care his health deteriorated leading to his discharge from the RAF in December 1942, suffering from tuberculosis. His health continued to decline until his death on 9th June 1947. At the time of his award, he was the youngest recipient of a Victoria Cross in World War II, and he remains the youngest ever recipient of a Victoria Cross awarded in respect of aerial operations.

Marshall of the Royal Air Force, Lord Trenchard, visited the station on 17 April 1941 in what his biographer, Alan Boyle, has described as his self-appointed role of Inspector General. His Lordship gave his customary lecture on morale to all ranks before a Mess Dinner in his honour which was attended by the Earl and Countess of Stair.

When the war commenced in September 1939, the RAF did not have men trained in airfield defence. A new trade, 'Ground Gunner', was introduced and training commenced immediately. Until these men became available, assistance in airfield defence was obtained from the army. It is believed that West Freugh was helped by a detachment of Royal Scots Fusiliers from their depot in Ayr. By October 1940 when 35,000 trained men were available, Ground Defence Flights were formed, one of which took up duty at West Freugh. On 6th January 1942, the RAF Regiment was formed, and all ground defence units were incorporated into the Regiment from 1st February 1942. Unfortunately records of Regiment units at training airfields have not been retained by the Public Records Office. However, the RAF Regiment Association advises that 2784 Squadron was formed at West Freugh from the existing ground defence Flights.

Older aircraft types used by the School were phased out as soon as possible; by April 1940 Fairey Battle numbers had increased to twenty-four. The Rolls Royce Merlin engined Battle which had been a front-line medium bomber at the outbreak of war had now been relegated to Training Command where it was used mainly as a target tug.

In April 1941 re-equipment with Blackburn Bothas commenced. The Unit establishment was to become sixty-six Bothas and twenty-seven Battles, with the Battles, together with a number of Lysanders, restricted in use to target towing for air to air gunnery practice. The Botha which had two 880 hp Bristol Perseus engines had been withdrawn from operational use as it was underpowered. Now in a training role it was unpopular with aircrews. Ten Bothas were lost in flying accidents between 28th August 1941 and 1st October 1942. However they continued in use until gradually replaced by Avro Ansons from April 1942. The Anson with two 310 hp Armstrong Siddeley Cheetah engines was widely used by Training Command. Seven thousand Ansons were supplied to the RAF between 1936 and 1950.

130 Squadron, Fighter Command, based at Perranporth near Newquay, Cornwall, were advised on 1 August 1942 that they were to be released from operational duties to take part in an army co-operation exercise. A ground party left by road the same day to travel to West Freugh. Next morning eighteen Supermarine Spitfire Vbs flew north to Colerne, near Bath where they were delayed by bad weather until 4 August when they flew to Woodvale near Liverpool to refuel. They took off to fly to West Freugh but weather conditions forced them to divert to Valley near Holyhead on the island of Anglesey before they were able to continue to West Freugh where they arrived in the early evening.

On 5 August the Squadron was at readiness at 8.30 am to take part in a large-scale exercise involving two army Divisions who were defending Scotland against attack along a line running due east from Ayr. For the purpose of the exercise the Squadron represented enemy aircraft carrying out low level attacks on advancing columns of troops. Four attacks each involving eight Spitfires were carried out that day and a further three sorties on the following day though weather conditions were poor for the low level attacks required. From 7 August the weather precluded any flying before the exercise ended at 2 pm on 9 August. On 10 August with at length some improvement in weather conditions, all eighteen aircraft carried out formation flying practice around West Freugh during the afternoon. The villagers in Sandhead and Stoneykirk no doubt found this display of greater interest than the routine Ansons and Bothas which did not merit a second glance.

On 11 August in now perversely perfect weather the eighteen Spitfires flew direct from West Freugh to Perranporth completing the trip in less than two hours. At the end of November 1942 the personnel complement of the School was 1,370 men and 430 women and the aircraft complement sixty-two Ansons and three Lysanders.

In June 1943 came another change of name to 4 (Observer) Advanced Flying Unit. The aircrew trade of Observer had previously been superseded by two new trades - Navigator and Bomb Aimer - necessitated by the change in style of bombing operations with the larger aircraft now in use. The Unit now concentrated on advanced training for both new trades with the greatest possible despatch. Trainees arriving at the Unit had completed basic training to obtain their aircrew brevets; most held the rank of Sergeant, some were commissioned as Pilot Officers. Many were from Australia, Canada and other Commonwealth countries where many of the RAF trainees had also trained under the Empire Air Training Scheme.

Navigation training concentrated on gaining experience in cross country flying on trips of three to three and one half hours duration by day and by night using dead reckoning navigation techniques aided by map reading, wireless direction finding and, as they became available, Gee and other radar navigational aids.

Much of the training of Bomb Aimers was in practice, using eleven pound smoke bombs, over targets which had been set up in Luce Bay and a number of inland targets usually situated on stretches of moorland with no adjacent habitation. Each target had two nearby sighting posts from which quadrant bearings were taken on each bomb burst to assess the accuracy of aim. The two Luce Bay targets were erected in 1937 by the contractors who had constructed the airfield. They were situated at the shallow northern end of the bay, built on the sandy sea bed offshore, but above the low water mark. Considerable difficulty was found in ensuring the stability of the three conical supports required to carry each triangular target platform which had to be above sea level in all conditions. Eventually, foundations were taken to a depth of 30 feet, no easy task working between tides using the limited construction material then available. The measure of their success is shown by the fact that in 1999 the remains of both targets can still be seen.

Navigators and Bomb Aimers were given a good grounding, and practice, in each other's skills and both trades were given training and experience in air to air gunnery. In February 1942 flying hours in training were 1,226; in November this had increased to 3,558 and in July 1943 to 4,196 hours. By April 1944 with a less urgent demand for aircrews, flying hours for the month had fallen to 2,698.

Inevitably with this volume of flying, accidents occurred; over twenty fatal accidents involving aircraft from the Unit were recorded between 1939 and 1945. Following normal RAF practice, help was given on a number of occasions when aircraft from other units came to grief in the vicinity of West Freugh. The most serious involved a US Air Force plane. On 27 July 1944 a Douglas C47A Dakota Air Ambulance of 301 Troop Carrier Squadron, 9th US Air Force Command, crashed into cliffs four miles south of Portpatrick whilst flying from Southampton to Prestwick. An accompanying C47A landed at West Freugh to raise the alarm. A search and rescue party soon located the wreckage but there were no survivors. In addition to a crew of five the C47A was carrying thirteen wounded soldiers from Normandy who were being repatriated to the United States together with a Nursing Sister, two medical orderlies and an RAF Leading Aircraftsman. The RAF man was going on leave to his home at Kilwinning, close to Prestwick - he had scrounged a lift.

West Freugh records show that, having located the crash, twenty-two bodies were recovered with the aid of the Portpatrick lifeboat. The Royal National Lifeboat Institution report, published in 1946, records that after being called out at 6 pm the lifeboat *Jeanie Spiers* reached the crash site at Cairngarroch Bay some four miles south of Portpatrick in "fine weather with a slight north-west breeze and a calm sea". They were the first to reach the scene where they found "a Dakota Air Ambulance had struck the cliff as it came in from the sea. The foreshore was littered with the bodies of the American soldiers who had been aboard". As the accident site was inaccessible by land the RAF rescue party requested assistance from the RNLI to recover the bodies; with darkness now approaching this was left until the following day. On 16th August, RNLI Headquarters announced a reward of £22 to the lifeboat crew.

The US Army Air Forces Accident Report dated 31 July states that weather conditions were "five to six tenths cloud with cloud base of eight hundred feet, visibility ten miles with patches of sea fog". The nature of the accident is recorded as "plane crashed into 426 foot cliff lacking only 20 feet of clearing it".

Description of the accident says "due to low ceiling the pilot was forced to fly low to allow following plane to maintain visual contact. As he neared land it became necessary to pull up and go on instruments. He did not climb to a height which would clear the cliff which was hidden from sight. The following plane cleared it by only a few feet".

The six inches to one mile Ordnance Survey map shows that Cairngarroch Bay has a shoreline of about 750 yards wholly lined by cliffs which vary in height between 150 feet and 300 feet. The highest point in the vicinity is Bailie Hill some 800 yards inland which has an Ordnance Survey trigonometrical point at 425 feet.

Due largely to the considerable efforts of a local man, Mr S Rankin, the crash site has now been marked by an engraved plaque which was affixed before the 55th anniversary of the crash on 27 July 1999, when a commemorative service was held at the site. Mr Rankin contacted relatives of those who lost their lives, three of whom came from the US to attend the service. A wreath was laid by the sister of the Nursing Sister who perished. Also attending was the only surviving member of the Portpatrick Lifeboat crew which attended the crash.

Other flying accidents of lesser consequence were accepted as part of normal routine such as the Heyford which landed safely on 3 March 1940 after catching fire over Luce Bay when a bullet fired by one of its own guns pierced a wing petrol tank due to failure of a cut-out system on the gun mounting. There were no casualties though the aircraft was burned out. On 2 March 1943 a Lysander landed safely after "a seagull flew through the windscreen"; the pilot was treated for minor cuts and shock

In Stoneykirk Parish cemetery, a mile from and within sight of the airfield there are eighteen war graves in which are buried one Fleet Air Arm pilot, eight Royal Air Force aircrew members and nine aircrew of the Australian, Canadian and New Zealand Air Forces.

Because of its location 50 miles south of the wartime Transatlantic Terminal at Prestwick several cross-Atlantic flights which had gone slightly astray landed at West Freugh. The first was a Lockheed Hudson which landed on 15 June 1941 after a direct flight from Newfoundland. In ensuing months there were other unexpected arrivals including on 9 November 1942 a Douglas Boston completing a cross-Atlantic trip which, having called on an emergency wireless frequency, landed so short of fuel that both engines cut out on the approach. On 17 April 1943 a Boeing Flying Fortress, also short of fuel, rather than make a circuit landed downwind causing it to run off the end of the runway, fortunately without damage.

When the war in Europe ended on 8 May 1945 training of aircrews ceased almost immediately and 4 (O) AFU was disbanded on 21 June 1945. No figures are available but a conservative estimate suggests that over two thousand Observers, Navigators and Bomb Aimers had been trained since the outbreak of war.

8. Westland Wallace, 1 Anti-Aircraft Co-operation Unit, West Freugh. 28th May, 1938   RAFM P8826

9. McDonnell Phantoms, 143 Squadron, West Freugh, during Operation Purple Warrior. 14th November, 1987.
MODPW500

10. Boeing Chinook II, engaged in Operation Green Blade, Castle Kennedy. November, 1994   GG429

CHAPTER 4

WEST FREUGH IN THE 1990's

In April 1991 the then newly formed Space Department of the Defence Research Agency opened a Satellite Station which had been built at West Freugh by Siemens Plessey Ltd. The major item of equipment at the station is a 43 foot diameter antenna housed in a large 'golf ball' radome. The station was sited at West Freugh in order that it could be well away from any likely source of interference and have an unobstructed view down to the horizon. A second newly installed and slightly smaller Radome became operational in mid 1999 at which time all operations by the Defence Evaluation Research Agency Space Department (DERA) were transferred to West Freugh. DERA, with the headquarters of their Test and Evaluation Ranges Division based at Boscombe Down, became responsible for West Freugh in 1997.

Early in 1992 the Dumfries and Galloway Aviation Museum, which is housed in the former air traffic control building of RAF Station Heathhall, Dumfries, inserted an advertisement in local newspapers throughout Great Britain seeking a response from anyone who had wartime service with any of the RAF Units in Dumfries and Galloway who might be interested in attending a reunion which the Museum proposed to organise.

The response was described as 'quite frankly, astounding', arrangements went ahead and a reunion was held on 6th and 7th June. On Saturday 6th June a large number of veterans, many accompanied by husbands or wives and families, assembled at the Museum where a Memorial plaque was unveiled with due ceremony before a Spitfire XIX from the Battle of Britain Memorial Flight 'beat up' the crowd around the Museum building.

On Saturday 7th June, some 70 enthusiastic veterans and family members set off from Dumfries on a coach tour of former bases in Galloway. First point of call was Gibb Hill, Kirkcudbright, where some of the former Air Sea Rescue buildings, now in industrial use, are just recognisable. At Wigtown and Castle Kennedy the only visible signs now are hangars housing a variety of stores, workshops etc.

In Stranraer, buildings such as Craignelder and North West Castle were recognised though much changed in appearance since their days in RAF occupation. Other than two large slipways and a number of hard standings formerly used by flying boats under maintenance, little remains to be seen at Wig Bay.

The final call was at West Freugh, the only airfield in Dumfries and Galloway which remains in use though no longer occupied by the RAF. The party was welcomed by senior members of the MOD management team and were given a guided tour of the airfield allowing those who had served at 'Wet Through' as the station was commonly known (a comment on the prevailing winter weather) to recognise hangars and many wooden buildings looking much as they had almost fifty years earlier.

A photograph showing the group standing alongside a Buccaneer aircraft in one of the hangars is to be seen on page 40.

Despite changes in control of the airfield over a period of almost seventy years the outward appearance of West Freugh has changed very little. As the visiting veterans found, the seven pre-war Bellman hangars remain, having been re-clad between late 1993 and March 1994. Both original runways remain in use having been re-laid and resurfaced to meet present standards and having been equipped with modern safety devices such as arrester gear and safety nets. In this context it is worth noting that virtually all modern high speed fighter/bombers e.g. the Tornado are fitted with arrester hooks as standard.

As noted in chapter 6 the Royal Aerospace Establishment assumed responsibility for the airfield when the Bombing trials Unit was disbanded at the end of June 1959. From this date running of the airfield was 'fully contractorised'. The present contractor is required to operate the airfield and ranges in accordance with Ministry of Defence requirements and instructions. All equipment, aircraft, vehicles, instrumentation, etc. is Ministry of Defence funded. Management and overall control of West Freugh is by Procurement Executive staff. Security is enforced by Ministry of Defence Police.

The contractor is wholly responsible for Air Traffic Control including associated radar systems together with range control and safety radar. Air traffic control radar with a range in excess of fifty miles uses a transmitter in the middle of the airfield. Range radar uses two transmitters, the southern end of the range is viewed from the coastline at Drummore and the remainder by a transmitter on the northern end of the range close to the airfield. Screens in the control room alongside the northern transmitter enable one operator to view the whole range.

A prime responsibility is the control and operation of four transportable Electro-Optical Trackers used when required during weapons trials over the Luce Bay Range. These trackers can then be transported along public highways to any required location in the vicinity of the range then on arrival rapidly positioned with a geographic location accurate to within a few millimetres. An aircraft detected at extreme range can be tracked with progress recorded on video tape and also filmed by complex high speed cine cameras using 650 metre film reels. A bomb or projectile leaving the aircraft can be tracked and filmed until the point of impact with the target. When processed each cine-film frame can be examined individually thus allowing detailed analysis.

Two ranges, Luce Bay and North Channel remain in use. Sea and land targets are available within the Luce Bay range which has an area of 380 square kilometres. On land a large soft target area and a larger hard target area, both with full optical instrumentation are available within a littoral land area which includes eight kilometres of beach. Non-specular laser targets can be deployed when required.

The North Channel range with an area of 240 square kilometres is used for quality control and evaluation testing of Sonobuoys using a computer controlled semi-automatic test procedure. Until April 1994 these buoys were flown and dropped over the range by two veteran De Havilland Devon aircraft based at West Freugh. The Devons were replaced by a former Royal

Navy British Aerospace Jetstream, a twin turboprop aircraft with a cruising speed of 264 knots which is still in use and is now the only Ministry of Defence aircraft based at West Freugh. It is anticipated that the Jetstream will be withdrawn during Summer 2000 to be replaced by a Rotary Wing Aircraft. Two British Aerospace Buccaneers which were based at West Freugh for some years for use over the ranges flown by RAF aircrews as and when required were withdrawn early in 1995.

British Aerospace Flying College Ltd operated a pilot training school at Prestwick Airport which is some fifty miles north of West Freugh. In summer months when their work load was heavy, British Aerospace, by arrangement with the Ministry of Defence used West Freugh to extend their training capacity. Pupils and instructors were flown in on a day to day basis flying Piper Warriors or Swiss built FAA Bravo single engined training aircraft. However for what are understood to be economic reasons British Aerospace have now moved all pilot training to an airfield in Spain.

Military exercises involving the use of West Freugh facilities have been held from time to time. One such exercise, named 'Green Blade', held for two weeks in November 1994 was described as a 'Support Helicopter Training Exercise' which required simulation of rescue of hostages and evacuation of British expatriates from a war torn Third World country. Some 440 soldiers and 1100 airmen were involved, many of them accomodated at the former RAF airfield at Castle Kennedy. Thirty helicopters, the largest number in any one area since the Gulf War in 1992, took part. Boeing Chinook II's, Westland Pumas and a few Westland Gazelles flew from Castle Kennedy and from 'advanced bases', for example four Pumas were flown for several days from the Forestry Commission Caravan Site at Talnotry near New Galloway. A number of the Chinooks and Pumas were from 18 Squadron based at Laarbruch, Germany. Others were from Odiham, Hampshire.

Also involved were British Aerospace Hawks from 100 Squadron based at Finningley, Yorkshire, which, operating in flights of three, tested helicopter crews defensive and evasive techniques. West Freugh was used by Lockheed Hercules from Lyneham, Wiltshire making supply and evacuation flights on a daily basis.

More recently, West Freugh played a part in 'a large scale airmobile field training excercise' named 'Corsican Lanyard' whichwas carried out between 17 May and 27 May 1999 by 5 Airborne Brigade based at Aldershot. West Freugh acted as a base from which a number of operations involving Hercules aircraft together with Chinook and Puma helicopters were launched. The helicopters also used part of the former Castle Kennedy airfield as a base.

It is understood that the Ministry of Defence intend to continue using the airfield and range facilities at West Freugh for the foreseeable future. The most recent advice is that it is planned that in 2001 DERA will become a plc, partly Government owned with the company being floated on the stock market to inject capital for investment etc. Under these conditions West Freugh would still be owned by the Ministry of Defence but staff members would no longer enjoy civil servant status.

11. Type 3 High Speed Launch

RAFM P7357

12. Luce Bay Floating Target moored in Drummore Harbour   *Author*

13. Range Vessel Aquila Maris, Portpatrick Harbour.   *Author*

14. World War II Veterans and families alongside a Buccaneer at West Freugh. 7th June, 1992   *T.E.E.*

CHAPTER 5

ANTI-AIRCRAFT CO-OPERATION

In addition to 4 (O) AFU other units were housed at West Freugh from 1938 onwards.

In Spring 1938 an Anti-Aircraft Training Camp was opened at Burrowhead south of Isle of Whithorn to train Royal Artillery Territorial soldiers in the use of 3.7 inch heavy anti-aircraft guns. Targets for firing and range finding practice were provided by aircraft-towed drogues. From 19 April 1938 E Flight of 1 Anti Aircraft Co-operation Unit flying Westland Wallace target-towing planes was based at West Freugh until 15 September 1938 when the Territorial Army Camp season ended.

On 3 April 1933 a Westland Wallace flown by Flight Lieutenant D F McIntyre accompanied a Westland PV3 piloted by the Marquis of Clydesdale on the first ever flight over Mount Everest.

On 1 May 1939 the same Flight, now flying Hawker Henleys, returned to West Freugh to resume co-operation with 2 Heavy Anti Aircraft Practice Camp which was now a permanent unit. The Henley was originally produced as a light bomber to the same Air Ministry specification as the Fairey Battle and was considered by many to be the better aircraft - it was faster and could carry a greater bomb load than the Battle. However the Air Ministry decided that Henleys should be used only as target tugs. Two hundred were built, each equipped with a 1020 hp Rolls Royce Merlin engine giving a maximum speed with a drogue in tow of 270 mph.

In October 1939 one modified Boulton Paul Defiant with its gun turret removed was added to the Flight as a towing aircraft.

All target towing aircraft were now being given distinctive

markings in an endeavour to ensure that other aircraft avoided the risk of hitting a fine diameter tow wire attached to a drogue which could be over one mile behind the towing aircraft. The undersides of all target tugs were painted in the standard Training Command brilliant yellow colouring with, for these aircraft, the addition of broad black diagonal stripes. It is perhaps significant that despite the hundreds of hours flown by target tugs at West Freugh, Castle Kennedy and Wigtown airfields, there are no recorded flying accidents involving collision with a tow cable.

In November 1942 the Flight was taken over by 289 Squadron based at Turnhouse, Edinburgh, which had detachments on AA co-operation duties at several airfields. Henleys were now entirely replaced by Defiants until June 1943 when they in turn were replaced by Miles Martinets. The Martinet, a development of the Miles Master, was the first RAF aircraft to be designed specifically as a target tug. With an 870 hp Bristol Mercury engine it had a maximum speed of 240 mph.

In July 1943 a Hawker Hurricane was added to the Flight to provide "high speed silent practice" for the gunners, that is no shots were fired, the guns being fitted with cine-camera recording devices.

On 18 January 1944 and again on 7 March 1944 Martinets crashed into the sea between West Freugh and Burrowhead. In both cases pilot and winch operator were killed.

In March 1945 two Vultee Vengeance aircraft joined the West Freugh detachment. Designed in the US as a dive bomber the only RAF use in Great Britain was for target towing. Flying time recorded in March 1945 was 307 hours; as the time from West Freugh to Burrowhead for the Hurricane and Vengeance was only a matter of moments this would mean about 250 hours spent "over the guns". Some time was necessarily taken by the Vengeance to deploy the drogue target which, for safety reasons, was normally towed at a distance of from 6,000 to 8,000 feet.

In June 1945 289 Squadron was disbanded. The four Vengeance IV and two Hurricane IIIC aircraft then based at West Freugh were designated 1353 Flight, Fighter Command. In July 1945 training courses at Burrowhead ceased; from then on all co-operation was with AA Training Camps and Searchlight Units in north east England and in Northern Ireland. Three Spitfire XVIs were added to the Flight in mid-August 1945 before the Flight eventually left West Freugh on 31 January 1946 on transfer to Turnhouse.

CHAPTER 6

BOMBING TRIALS UNIT

In mid 1941 Bomber Command Experimental Unit based at Boscombe Down, Wiltshire were authorised to arrange construction of a target which would allow realistic trials of bombs and bombing techniques. This target was built at Braid Fell twelve miles from West Freugh on moorland 600 feet above Loch Ryan between Innermessan and New Luce close to where Penwhirn Reservoir now stands. A factory building believed to be similar to many in the Ruhr was erected. It consisted of three adjacent blocks of one, two and three storeys, each block 80 feet by 200 feet, with a concrete apron 120 feet by 200 feet. A steel girder framework was completed by reinforced concrete and brickwork; one block had a flat roof, the others ridged roofs using slates, tiles and corrugated sheeting.

Building work having been completed in August 1941, three Handley-Page Hampden bombers were detached from Boscombe Down to West Freugh together with thirty-eight personnel from the Experimental Unit. Bombing trials commenced immediately and continued until April 1942 when they were suspended to allow substantial repairs to be undertaken to the badly damaged target. Meantime trials continued using the pre-war Luce Bay ranges now increased in area and augmented with additional targets.

At this point the Armament Directorate of the Ministry of Aircraft Production took an interest. Within a few weeks the West Freugh detachment, with the same aircraft and personnel was designated the Bombing Trials Unit with a Wing Commander in charge who reported directly to the Ministry of Aircraft Production.

In May 1942 the Bombing Trials Unit sought approval for a unit crest similar in style to that in use by 4 Air Observer School. The Inspector of RAF Badges duly approved a crest with an emblem consisting of 'A mailed fist dexter clutching a bomb' with the motto 'Search and Research'.

Trials at Braid Fell recommenced in July 1942 to continue there and on Luce Bay ranges throughout the war years during which time the original Hampdens were replaced by North American Mitchell, Handley Page Halifax, Avro Lancaster and De Havilland Mosquito bombers. Hampdens remained in occasional use, one of the original three, P1216, crashed on Braid Fell on 18 January 1944.

From time to time other units were involved in specific trials. An example arose when a series of tests were required to assess bomb casings designed to contain a greater high explosive charge. Preliminary trials undertaken by BTU Hampdens dropping inert bombs having proved inconclusive it was decided to carry out further tests dropping bombs with a full high explosive charge but without fuses. When approached by the Ministry of Aircraft Production for assistance, Bomber Command allocated 617 Squadron - the Dam Busters - to carry out these tests as part of their normal routine training programme. The Squadron was based at Coningsby in Lincolnshire under command of Wing Commander Leonard Cheshire. Between 18 October 1943 and 22 April 1944 617 Squadron bombed the Braid Fell target on fourteen occasions, dropping 120 x 500 lb, 34 x 1000 lb and 14 x 4000 lb bombs, a total of 168 bombs weighing over 65 tons. Thirty-six or 21% were direct hits, twenty or 12% fell within five yards of the target. For the technically minded, all fourteen exercises were carried out in daylight hours by Avro Lancaster 1 aircraft flying at 14,000 feet at an indicated airspeed of 175 mph using a Mk IIA Semi Automatic Bomb Sight. The test series was completed when on 3 April 1944 six Mosquitoes of 8 Pathfinder Force Group each dropped one 4000 lb bomb then finally in August 1944 a BTU Halifax from West Freugh dropped a further twenty 500 lb bombs. Though unfused, a few bombs exploded on impact posing some risk to the ground observers who logged the precise location of each bomb as it fell to allow it to be dug out for examination by Ministry of Aircraft Production experts.

After collection and analysis by these ballistic experts, the trial results were passed to a team led by Barnes Wallis of 'bouncing bomb' fame, whose work culminated in the introduction of the 12000lb Grand Slam bombs which were used with devastating effect during the last twelve months of the war, in particular by 617 Squadron bombing precision targets, flying modified Lancaster III bombers.

When 4(O) AFU was disbanded in June 1945, BTU continued to operate from West Freugh carrying out tests on a wide range of armaments, pyrotechnics and other equipment including airborne radar.

With the end of the war large numbers of surplus aircraft required storage pending disposal. Space at West Freugh not in use by BTU was taken over by 57 Maintenance Unit, Wig Bay, from July 1945 until June 1947 to store surplus Mosquitoes, up to eighty-five being stored at any one time. Most were sold as scrap, a few were overhauled before sale to the Air Forces of France, Belgium and Turkey.

Another unit housed at West Freugh for a time was the West of Scotland Hospital which moved here when the RAF Hospital at Lochnaw closed down in October 1945. The Hospital, which had a specialised surgical unit, closed down on 30 November 1949.

Meantime BTU was temporarily transferred to RAF Station Wigtown from June 1947 until May 1948. At this time the personnel strength was 130 with a Squadron Leader in command. Aircraft in use were three Avro Lancaster IIIs, two De Havilland Mosquitoes and one Hawker Tempest.

The Unit had, since the end of 1945, been responsible for the Mountain Rescue Unit which had operated from Wigtown since 1942 and whose services were still occasionally required. An instance occurred on 11 April 1947 when they were called upon to recover the bodies of six crew members from a Royal Belgian Air Force Douglas Dakota which had crashed on the previous day at Carlin's Cairn some four miles south west of Carsphairn whilst flying from Brussels to Prestwick. Regular exercises were carried out; one in November 1947 encountered severe weather conditions, wind gusts of 100 mph being recorded at a height of 2,700 feet on the Merrick, the highest peak in the Southern Uplands. On 18 August 1949 another exercise on moorland adjacent to the Braid Fell range involved two RAF dogs which had been flown in with their handlers from Spaverton near Cheltenham.

Shortly after return to West Freugh in May 1948 BTU was supplied with two Avro Lincolns with which trials continued on the Luce Bay and Braid Fell ranges. Items tested included incendiary clusters, fragmentation bombs, 4000 lb high explosive bombs, rockets, stabilised automatic bomb sights, Gee radar and H2S radar. Bombs were dropped from heights varying from 500 feet to 28,000 feet.

During 1951 aircraft in use were three Lincolns and one Mosquito in addition to several North American Harvards (four were in use at one time) which were used for communications and also for pilot training; for example all of the Unit pilots used the Harvards for ground controlled approach training using facilities which were made available at RAF Prestwick. The twin seat Harvard with a 550 hp Pratt and Whitney Wasp engine had been flying with the RAF since 1938; principally in a pilot training role, though now reaching the end of their service, a few continued in use into the 1960s. Those in use at West Freugh were replaced in August 1951 by one Avro Anson.

By 1952 targets in Luce Bay included a Drifter used as a "very high level" bombing target.

In April 1953 the Unit, now commanded by a Squadron Leader, had a strength of four Lincolns, one Mosquito and one Anson. The serviceability of the Lincoln aircraft created problems; there are regular comments on the problems caused by the shortage of spares which meant that frequently only one Lincoln was in serviceable condition.

In 1954 anti-submarine charges were tested off Killiness Point near Drummore. During March 1954 a number of 10,000 lb bombs were dropped over a period of four days on a specially prepared target in Luce Bay. It is on record that during 1955 and 1956 the Bomber wing of 2 Tactical Air Force, comprising 102, 103, 104 and 149 Squadrons flying English Electric Canberra 2s from Gutersloh in Germany bombed targets in Luce Bay from heights of between 40 000 and 48 000 feet using radar sighting techniques. The Braid Fell range was de-requisitioned in April 1960 after last being used in late 1958. During the last few years of use, a siren was sounded to clear the area each time the target was used. Before final closure a bomb disposal team spent several weeks ensuring that the whole site was completely clear of explosives before it was returned to the original owners. This did not prevent in April 1990 an agricultural contractor using a JCB to carry out excavations at Braid Fell unearthing a 500 lb bomb which had lain dormant for around forty years. An RAF bomb disposal team from Cambridgeshire carried out a controlled explosion to safely dispose of this relic.

In August 1957 an English Electric Canberra B2 joined the Unit, the first pure jet aircraft to be used. The Canberra B2, which was later replaced by a Canberra B6, was a light bomber with a crew of three equipped with two Rolls Royce Avon 101 jet engines.

At the beginning of 1958 the Unit personnel strength was twenty officers and one hundred and ten airmen, having dropped from a total of 300 in May 1956, by the end of the year this had fallen to fifteen officers and fifty-five airmen. On 30 June 1959 the Bombing Trials Unit was formally closed down. The remaining personnel were transferred to other units.

Armament testing and developing work now passed to the Royal Aircraft Establishment, since renamed the Royal Aerospace Establishment, which is part of the Procurement Executive of the Ministry of Defence. They now took over control of the West Freugh establishment.

Weapon development trials continued such as those on airborne missiles test-fired by Hawker-Siddeley Buccaneer aircraft. During the 1960s and 1970s ranges now covering the greater part of Luce Bay which is the largest bay in Scotland, and a further two hundred and fifty square miles of the North Channel west of Portpatrick, were used for trials involving Canberra and Avro Vulcan bombers. Trials of weapon systems including Skybolt, Sea Eagle and Martel were also undertaken. In recent years Jaguars, Phantoms and Tornadoes of the RAF together with F111s and A10s of the US Air Force and other Nato forces have used the ranges to develop high speed, low level attack techniques. None of the aircraft now using the ranges are based at West Freugh; many are on training flights from RAF bases in the United Kingdom or in Europe. In March 1991 the Aeroplane and Armament Experimental Establishment at Boscombe Down, Wiltshire, confirmed that they use the West Freugh ranges.

For some time the airfield has been civilian staffed; the Royal Aerospace Establishment assumed responsibility for West Freugh in 1957. Civilian staff were employed progressively with tasks being taken over by contractors until by mid-1982 the airfield and ranges had become 'a fully contactorised establishment with only a small Procurement Executive management and supervisory team.' However for two weeks in November 1987 West Freugh became the Land Headquarters for one of two opposing forces taking part in Operation Purple Warrior, the largest military exercise to have been held in Great Britain for many years.

Throughout the exercise the airfield was in constant use by a wide variety of aircraft including British Aerospace Harrier; Lockheed Hercules; McDonnell Phantom; Sepecat Jaguar and Panavia Tornado planes together with Boeing Chinook and Westland Sea King Helicopters.

In April 1988 the Ministry of Defence announced that as part of a £30 million project to improve trial ranges, West Freugh would be provided with new tracking and sea surveillance radar, communications systems, radar data recorders and other equipment. Future use of the ranges was said to be likely to involve drop trials of stand-off missiles and new anti-radar and anti-tank missiles.

In November 1988 a Scottish newspaper reported that "runway cratering bombs" were under test at West Freugh ranges. This was presumably a reference to the JP233 bombs delivered by Tornado GR1 bombers which received considerable media attention in early reports on the Gulf War.

15. Factory Bombing Target, Braid Fell.   *PRO AIR 14/978*

16. Supermarine Stranraer Flying Boats   *Wigtown Museum service*

CHAPTER 7

RAF STATION, STRANRAER

On 20 August 1928 a meeting of Stranraer Town Council discussed and agreed to a request from the Air Ministry to place flying boat moorings in Loch Ryan adjacent to Stranraer Harbour. Some three weeks later on 7 September an RAF Supermarine Southampton flying boat left Falmouth, Cornwall for Lough Neagh in Northern Ireland. From there it flew to Loch Ryan arriving on 9 September and leaving next day for Lake Windermere. On board were a Royal Navy Commander accompanied by an RAF Wing Commander and two Flight Lieutenants who were to make on-the-spot assessments then report to the Air Ministry on the suitability of the sites visited for use by flying boats.

Little future use was made of Lough Neagh except for occasional use by flying boats of bombing and gunnery ranges on the Lough. However for a period of six months in 1944 Sandy Bay at the eastern side of the Lough became the United Kingdom terminal for supply flights by Consolidated Coronados of the US Naval Transport Service flying from New York via Newfoundland. Lake Windermere had been used during World War I by the Royal Naval Air Service who had a seaplane base at Hill of Oaks. Little subsequent use appears to have been made until Short Brothers established a Sunderland production line at Bowness-on-Windermere during World War II.

The report made on Loch Ryan must have been favourable as in the ten years between 1929 and the commencement of World War II in August 1939 flying boats from all home-based Squadrons visited Loch Ryan regularly on training exercises. No permanent base was set up, Loch Ryan being, in RAF jargon, an "advanced alighting area".

When required, local services were employed; boatmen were engaged to transport crews between anchorages and piers. Aircraft refuelling was carried out manually using four gallon petrol cans which were also transported by local boatmen. Aviation fuel was brought in by rail tanker to a designated siding at Stranraer Town railway station. Visiting aircrews were accommodated in hotels and airmen were billeted with local families until RAF accommodation became available when West Freugh airfield opened in January 1937. Occasionally flying boats which required more than the routine maintenance normally undertaken whilst afloat were beached on the foreshore adjacent to the harbour to allow overhaul to be carried out.

Following one or two earlier short visits the first flying boats to make full use of the Loch Ryan facilities were four Supermarine Southamptons of 201 Squadron which flew in from Invergordon on 31 August 1929 to spend six days on exercises before departing for Pembroke Dock. The Southampton was a twin engine biplane with two 502 hp Napier Lion engines. Designed by R. J. Mitchell it had a range of 500 miles. It carried a crew of five who were housed in four open cockpits, two in the nose carried two pilots and a navigator and two in the rear fuselage housed two fitters who were also trained gunners. Sixty eight Southamptons were supplied to the RAF between 1925 and 1936.

209 Squadron, Coastal Area Command, was formed at Mount Batten, Plymouth in January 1930. It was equipped with four Blackburn Iris MkIII flying boats. The Iris was a biplane with three 675 hp Rolls Royce Condor engines which, carrying a crew of five, gave a range of under 500 miles and an endurance of five hours. On 20 May 1930 Iris S1263 left Mount Batten on her first cruise - Naval terminology was regularly used in flying boat Squadron reports. The direct flight from Mount Batten to Loch Ryan was accomplished in four hours fifteen minutes. During the next seven days return flights were made from Loch Ryan to Donaghadee, Belfast and Tobermory before returning to Mount Batten, via Pembroke Dock, on 28 May. The objects of this cruise were recorded as - coastal pilot training; navigation; photography; working from an advanced base.

Four weeks later Iris S1263 accompanied by Iris S1264 flew to Reykjavic to moor alongside a Royal Navy Cruiser attending celebrations of the one thousandth anniversary of the Icelandic Parliament. Leaving Mount Batten on 20 June 1930 they flew with overnight stops in Loch Ryan and Stornoway to arrive in Reykjavic on 23 June. Flying separately they made the return journey between 2 July and 7 July. On 3 July S1264 flying from Stornoway to Loch Ryan made a forced landing at Ross of Mull to effect temporary repairs to the starboard engine. After continuing the journey to Loch Ryan further repairs were carried out before departure for Mountbatten next day.

The same two aircraft made a further long distance flight in 1931 when they flew to Egypt via Gibraltar and Malta carrying Sir John Salmond, Chief of Air Staff, on a tour of inspection of RAF bases.

From 19 June to 8 July 1930 a Mobile Wireless Station mounted in RAF vehicles was operated from Stranraer to maintain contact with the two aircraft on their Icelandic trip. A Coastal Area Command report dated 11 August noted that Iris flying boats on an Icelandic cruise had achieved an average speed of 80 knots and a range of approximately 390 nautical miles. During 1931 and 1932 Southamptons of 201 and 204 Squadrons and Irises of 209 Squadron made several short visits to Loch Ryan between May and September; one Iris from 209 Squadron visited in February 1932 on a "winter cruise".

On 7 July 1932 and again on 2 June and 5 July 1933 Air Marshall Clark-Hill, Air Officer Commanding, Coastal Area Command, made one day visits to Loch Ryan flying from Command Headquarters, Lee-on-Solent in a Southampton of 201 Squadron. The Command Senior Air Staff Officer, Air Commodore Gill, also paid a one day visit on 7 June 1933 in a Southampton of 204 Squadron. These visits were apparently all part of an on-going inspection and assessment of all west coast flying boat anchorages.

From 9 August to 31 August 1932 209 Squadron now equipped with three Iris MkVI and three Southamptons visited from Mount Batten on a bombing and gunnery training exercise. From 4 September to 15 September and again from 24 September to 10

October Southamptons of 210 Squadron visited from Pembroke Dock for gunnery and bombing practice "over Lough Neagh". On 26 May 1934 the Duke of Gloucester left London to fulfil a number of engagements in Northern Ireland. He flew from London aboard "the Prince of Wales's new aeroplane". After landing at Barton Aerodrome near Manchester to refuel he flew to Portpatrick from where 'The Times' reported "they were escorted by a Squadron of RAF flying boats until reaching the Ulster coast".

The facts were a little more prosaic. On 24 May Blackburn Perth K3582 of 209 Squadron left Mount Batten on a cruise to Stornoway which was to be interrupted on both outward and return journeys to escort His Royal Highness across the North Channel. Arriving in Loch Ryan on 25 May K3852 took off the following afternoon to meet the royal aircraft some miles south of the Mull of Galloway from where they escorted His Royal Highness to Portpatrick then across the North Channel to the Ulster coast where they were met by "three bombing machines of the Ulster Squadron" who continued the escort to Belfast Airport, Aldergrove where they arrived at 8 pm.

After continuing the cruise to Stornoway K3582 returned to Loch Ryan on 30 May. On 1 June escort of the royal aircraft was taken over from the Ulster Bomber Squadron at the Ulster coast and continued over the North Channel then south to the vicinity of St Bees Head on the Cumberland coast. The return journey to Mount Batten was completed the following day.

The Blackburn Perth was a development of the Blackburn Iris; it carried a crew of five and was equipped with three 825 hp Rolls Royce Buzzard engines giving a range of 1200 miles and a speed of 130 mph. Only four were built all of which served with 209 Squadron between 1934 and 1937. The last production model of the Perth had a Vickers 37mm gun, which fired 100 1½ lb shells per minute, fitted in an extended nose. This probably gave this Perth a greater fire power than any other contemporary flying boat. With the exception of the slightly larger Short Sarafand - a six engined version of the Short Singapore - which did not go into Squadron service, the Perth was the largest of the many biplane flying boats which have been flown by the Royal Air Force.

17. Blackburn Iris III

18. Supermarine Stranraer, beached alongside Agnew Crescent, Stranraer.   *Mrs R. Reid*

When Southamptons of 240 Squadron visited Loch Ryan from Mount Batten between 18 July and 4 August 1934, Lough Neagh was again the location of bombing and gunnery practice.

On 5 June 1935 four Southamptons of 204 Squadron arrived from Cattewater, Plymouth to take part in a Naval exercise involving HMS Titania and the 5th Submarine Flotilla; however due to unfavourable weather the exercise was cancelled allowing the Squadron to return to base on 9 June. An anti-submarine exercise which did go ahead was held in the North Channel for two days commencing on 2 March 1937 with five Southamptons of 210 Squadron flying from Loch Ryan to participate.

The first Supermarine Stranraer to visit Loch Ryan was K7287 of 228 Squadron which visited from Pembroke Dock in July 1937 and again visited from Strangford Lough from 6 August to 9 August. Unconfirmed reports suggest that on both visits K7287 used the Wig Bay area of the loch and that senior officers aboard were considering the possibility of establishing a permanent base at Wig Bay.

K7287 was the first production model of the Stranraer which was designed by R J Mitchell who was later to design the Spitfire. A metal biplane with two 875 hp Bristol Pegasus engines, it carried a crew of six, had a range of 1,000 miles and an endurance of nine hours which was well in excess of other contemporary flying boats. Twenty-three were built for the RAF with whom it flew from 1936 until finally withdrawn from service on 30 October 1942. The last operational patrol was flown from Loch Ryan by 240 Squadron on 17 March 1941. Forty Stranraers were also built in Canada by Canadian Vickers for use by the Royal Canadian Air Force.

The first Saunders Roe Londons seen in Loch Ryan were four from 204 Squadron which flew in from Cattewater on 11 September 1937 remaining until 19 September for armament training. On this and all subsequent pre-war training visits by flying boats to Loch Ryan armament training was carried out under the auspices of 4 Armament Training School which had opened at West Freugh in January 1937. The London was a biplane with two 1,000 hp Bristol Pegasus engines. With a crew of six it had a range of 1,100 miles and an endurance of five-and-a-half hours.

On 22 May 1938 five Londons of 201 Squadron arrived in Loch Ryan followed later the same day by five Short Singapores of 209 Squadron thus forming the largest group of flying boats yet seen in the Loch. The Singapore was yet another biplane which at first sight appeared very similar to the now familiar Southamptons and Stranraers until close inspection revealed that it had four 560 hp Rolls Royce Kestrel engines which were mounted in tandem to drive two conventional and two pusher airscrews. It carried a crew of six, had a range of 1,000 miles and an endurance of six-and-a-quarter hours.

Before returning to their respective bases three aircraft from each Squadron took part in a flying display held at West Freugh to mark Empire Air Day on 28 May.

The entry for Stranraer Harbour in the 1938/39 edition of Lloyds Register of Shipping advises visiting vessels to avoid "eleven seaplane mooring buoys on a line North by West from the end of the West Pier to a distance of about 800 yards" and also "eleven seaplane mooring buoys in Wig Bay lying East and West about one mile from the shore".

On 22 May 1939 five Singapores from 209 Squadron arrived for a period of armament training which was interrupted when from 2 June to 4 June three Singapores were detached to Holyhead where they assisted in a search for HM Submarine Thetis. This submarine had been reported missing on 1 June whilst undergoing commissioning trials in Liverpool Bay. She was found by surface vessels to be lying on the sea bed fourteen miles off Great Orme Head. Of one hundred and three men aboard, many of them civilian employees of Vickers Armstrong who had built Thetis, only four were rescued alive. Later salvaged and, renamed Thunderbolt, she served with the Royal Navy until she was lost on 13 March 1943 when she was sunk by an enemy surface craft off Cape Milazzo, Sicily .

Routine training visits to Loch Ryan ceased with the outbreak of war in August 1939 though flying boats did continue to use Loch Ryan. One such visit came on 1 January 1940 when a Short Sunderland from 228 Squadron left Invergordon for Pembroke Dock. Encountering severe snow storms en route it was diverted to Loch

19. Maintenance crews working on Short Sunderland. 57 MUI Wig Bay 1944. The tail plane ladder was removed when servicing was completed.

IWM CH 859

20. Short Sunderland taking off.   IWM CH 842

Ryan. Immediately on arrival in Stranraer the captain was contacted by Provost G W McDowall who requested assistance in obtaining supplies of yeast. Stranraer and surrounding districts had been isolated by heavy snow storms and supplies of yeast for baking had been exhausted. Having obtained permission from Squadron Headquarters the Sunderland flew to Belfast on 2 January to pick up 500 lbs of yeast then return to Stranraer where it remained until 9 January before weather conditions allowed completion of the flight to Pembroke Dock.

The Short S25 Sunderland was the first four engine monoplane flying boat to go into Squadron service with Coastal Command. MkI Sunderlands were fitted with four Bristol Pegasus 965 h.p. engines; later MkII and MkIII versions had 1065 hp Bristol Pegasus XVIII engines which gave a range of three thousand miles and an endurance of up to fifteen hours. Seven hundred and thirty-nine were built for the RAF who flew them from 1938 until 1959 from bases around the world. Sunderland Marks IV and V are commented on in the chapter on 57 Maintenance Unit.

In mid-1940 significant changes in the use of Loch Ryan commenced. On 26 June the Flying Boat Training Squadron transferred from Calshot on Southampton Water to Stranraer with four Singapore III flying boats. Squadron Headquarters were set up at 37 Queen Street, Stranraer. They were followed on 29 July by 240 Squadron which transferred from Pembroke Dock with four Stranraer flying boats to take up operational duties which commenced on 30 July when three Stranraers flew on convoy escort over the Western Approaches. Squadron Headquarters were set up in The Kiosk, Portrodie, adjacent to the harbour.

On 1 August 1940 RAF Coastal Command established RAF Station Stranraer with Station Headquarters in Anne House, Bellevilla Road. On the same day North West Castle became the Station Officers Mess and the Masonic Hall an Airmens Mess.

These units together with Station Headquarters and other commandeered premises around Stranraer were guarded by men trained as Ground Gunners, who, in February 1942, were incorporated into the newly-formed RAF Regiment, the Stranraer defence Flights becoming 2752 Squadron.

From mid-October 209 Squadron based at Pembroke Dock had one or two of their Saunders Roe Lerwicks frequently detached to Stranraer for operational duties until on 10 December the full Squadron with a strength of twenty-six officers and one hundred and fifty-eight other ranks was transferred to Stranraer. The Lerwick was the only British built twin engine monoplane flying boat to be flown by the RAF. With a crew of six, two 1375 hp Bristol Hercules engines gave a range of 1,450 miles and an endurance of seven hours.

On 6 November a Lerwick from Stranraer spent six hours escorting a Royal Navy convoy consisting of *HMS Hood*, two cruisers and three destroyers out into the Western Approaches. The Clyde-built, 42,000 ton *Hood* was Britain's largest battleship. Six months later, on 24 May 1941, she was sunk off Greenland by the *Bismarck*.

On 12 January 1941 Lerwick L7264 sighted a surfaced U-Boat which immediately dived. Depth charges were dropped but despite five hours' searching no further sightings were made. L7266 made sightings on 19 January and again on 6 February but despite attacks with depth charges and bombs no further trace of either U-Boat was found.

On 22 February the Wing Commander in command of the Squadron, flying Lerwick L7263 with eleven crew members, failed to return from an anti-submarine patrol. Another Lerwick taking part in a search for L7263 made a forced landing some miles off Malin Head, Northern Ireland due to an airlock in petrol feed pipes. In calm sea conditions it was able to taxi on one engine towards the coastline until an RAF launch arrived to tow it in to Lough Foyle.

During an anti-submarine patrol on 8 March 1941 Lerwick L7266 sighted a Focke Wulf Condor flying low over the sea. When the Condor increased speed to climb towards cloud cover L7266 jettisoned depth charges in order also to increase speed but lost the Condor in cumulus cloud. The four engine Condor was used by the Luftwaffe for long range maritime reconnaissance usually operating from airfields in occupied Norway.

The Lerwick was not a conspicuously successful aircraft. Only twenty-one were built; the first production models were evaluated by 240 Squadron in June 1939 before 209 Squadron was equipped with them in December 1939. It was said to have unpleasant handling characteristics including lateral instability. 209 was the only Squadron to fly Lerwicks operationally except for a period of three months in the summer of 1942 when 422 Squadron Royal Canadian Air Force flew them on escort patrols over Arctic convoys to Russia.

Stranraers of 240 Squadron were also fully engaged on operational duties. In the week ending 12 August 1940 the four Squadron aircraft flew 248 hours on operational duties, an average of over eight hours each day for each aircraft, clearly a pressure which could not have been maintained. In the twelve months from the outbreak of war until 3 September 1940 the Squadron flew 5,495 hours. Flying over the North Channel on an anti-submarine patrol on 7 September, Stranraer K7292 was signalled by *SS Marsa* who advised that *HMS Godetia* had sunk following a collision; *Marsa* had twenty-two survivors aboard. K7292 searched for some time but no other survivors were seen. *HMS Godetia* was a 925 ton K Class Corvette which had been launched only four months earlier; her normal crew complement was eighty-five.

When flying over the Western Approaches boats or rafts carrying survivors from torpedoed ships were seen from time to time. The nearest surface vessel - frequently some distance away - was always contacted to ensure that survivors were picked up. On 18 October Stranraer K7292 sighted a lifeboat with over twenty men on board. Circling as low as possible the crew dropped a tin containing a message "going to get help - will be back soon - good luck". Destroyer *H36* which was seventeen miles away was contacted by signal lamp to be given the position of the lifeboat. Due to deteriorating visibility K7292 was unable to find the lifeboat again and was relieved when *H36* signalled that she had picked up twenty-five survivors just two hours after the first sighting had been made.

On 20 December 1940 Wing Commander R H Carter, OBE, DFC, was awarded the Distinguished Service Order for "services whilst with 240 Squadron".

In February 1941 both 209 and 240 Squadrons started to re-equip with Consolidated Catalina flying boats, one of which flown by a 240 Squadron crew under training crashed in Lough Erne, Northern Ireland on 12 March. The aircraft burned out with all of the crew losing their lives.

Catalinas, built in the United States, were supplied to the RAF under a lease-lend agreement and these were the first two Squadrons to fly them. An all-metal monoplane with two 1200 hp Pratt & Whitney Twin Wasp engines, the range of 4,000 miles and endurance of eighteen hours were the longest of any RAF flying boat. Fuel load for a standard eighteen hour flight was 1400 gallons. Several Catalinas of 210 Squadron operating from Sullom Voe on Arctic flights had additional fuel tanks installed increasing capacity to 1800 gallons. This extended the standard flight to 24 hours with a maximum endurance of 30 hours. By the end of the war over six hundred and fifty had been supplied to the RAF of which eleven were of an amphibian version.

On 27 March 1941, now fully equipped with Catalinas, both 209 and 240 Squadrons were transferred to Killadeas on Lough Erne.

Meantime the Flying Boat Training Squadron had been renamed 4 (Coastal) Operational Training Unit and was continuing to train aircrews in the particular requirements of operating flying boats which differed in many respects from the land-based aircraft in which they had learned their trades. A large part of the training had a distinct naval aspect, it was necessary to achieve a sound knowledge of seamanship in addition to airmanship. Flying boats had to be moored using boat hooks and anchors, so a knowledge of tides and the recognition of channels and of marker buoys was essential. A high standard of navigational skill was essential particularly as Radar navigational aids did not operate over the North Atlantic until late in the war years. GEE radar transmissions over the Western Approaches commenced in mid-1943, operational aircraft were equipped with GEE sets as soon as possible, followed by training unit aircraft.

Two interesting aircraft which spent several weeks undergoing crew training with the Unit in November and December 1941 were Golden Hind and Golden Fleece. These were two of

21. Short Sunderland at Battle of Britain Air Display, Wig Bay. 1950.

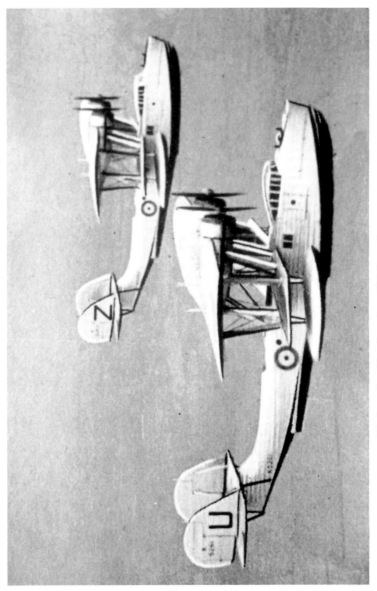

22. Saunders Roe London, 201 Squadron

23. Saro Lerwick, 209 Squadron RA. January, 1941   RAFM P811

three Short S26 flying boats which had been ordered by Imperial Airways   in 1938 only to be impressed for service with the RAF as soon as they were built. The third - Golden Horn - did not come to Stranraer before all three were attached to 119 Squadron at Loch Indal, Islay.

By April 1941 the strength of the Unit had increased to two Singapores, two Stranraers, two Londons, two Lerwicks and three Catalinas. From May 1941 Catalina training courses played an increasingly important part in the work of the Unit so much so that although the United States was not then involved in the war, three US Navy pilots were attached to the Unit in May 1941 as Catalina instructors.

In June 1941 4 (C) OTU was transferred to Invergordon though from March to November 1942 a detachment of seven Londons, three Catalinas and three Sunderlands returned to Stranraer where they concentrated on pilot training in order to ease pressure on training facilities at Invergordon.

During the time 4 (C) OTU spent at Stranraer four fatal flying accidents were recorded with twenty-three aircrew losing their lives.

Filling the gap left when 4 (C) OTU moved out, a Royal Canadian Air Force unit, 413 Squadron, was formed at Stranraer on 1 July 1941. By the end of July the Squadron was equipped with eight Catalinas with day and night flying training in full swing. Training, which included a limited number of operational flights, continued until the end of September when the Squadron transferred to Sullom Voe in the Shetlands to take up full operational duties. One Catalina crashed on take-off on 23 August with five crew members including a US Navy Ensign killed.

228 Squadron was the first Sunderland Squadron based in the Mediterranean, arriving in Malta at the end of 1940. They subsequently flew operationally from Alexandria, Khartoum, Leopoldsville, Lagos and Bathurst before arriving in Freetown, Sierra Leone where they were advised at the end of September 1941 that they were to return to Great Britain where they would re-form and re-equip at Stranraer. An advance party arrived at Stranraer in mid-October to take over accommodation recently

vacated by 413 Squadron. By mid-November with disembarkation leave completed the Squadron was fully re-formed at Stranraer to commence re-equipment and refresher training with Sunderland flying boats. Training completed, operational flying over the Western Approaches was carried out until 20 March 1942 when the Squadron transferred to Oban.

A narrative report on Coastal Command activities prepared by 15 Group - the Group which controlled operations from Stranraer and other Stations in the Western Approaches area - gives an insight into operational conditions. It describes how during 1941 obsolete biplanes were phased out leaving the Group with Sunderland and Catalina Squadrons. Both aircraft carried a crew of two pilots, the senior one as Captain, one navigator, three wireless operators, two fitters and two riggers. Wireless operators had specialised training in visual signalling by Aldis Lamp. Communication with shipping was necessarily in this way as wireless silence was mandatory to avoid alerting enemy ships or aircraft. Wireless operators, fitters and riggers were trained as air gunners and all crew members were trained in basic navigation by dead reckoning.

Whilst one engine fitter acted as flight engineer all fitters and riggers could carry out minor running repairs in flight. In an emergency leading to a forced landing it was frequently possible to make repairs enabling a safe return to base.

Patrols were usually of fourteen to eighteen hours' duration during which watch was changed every two hours; off duty crew had bunks on which they could rest. Galleys equipped with primus stoves allowed off-duty crew members to cook four hot meals with a total of 4,500 calories per man on patrols of over twelve hours. Hot drinks of tea or cocoa were taken every two hours.

A coastal command operational tour ended when 1000 hours flying with an operational unit had been logged. This at times meant changes being made in a crew as not all members had equal flying hours. The bomber command system of 30 operations to a tour was impracticable in Coastal Command.

Maintenance crews worked in difficult conditions. Engine inspections on Sunderlands were carried out working on a narrow platform twelve feet above the sea. Tools dropped could not be retrieved! Protection from the weather could not be given; there is no lee side as a moored flying boat always rides into wind. In winter months maintenance crews were usually relieved at hourly intervals.

Because of the geographic location Loch Ryan was a convenient arrival or departure point for transatlantic flying boat flights. RAF Station Stranraer consequently became host to a number of VIPs. The first such arrival recorded was on 15 September 1941 when a US Navy XPB2Y flying boat (a Catalina) arrived from Newfoundland with President Roosevelt's envoy W A Harriman accompanied by senior US military officers. The party were taken immediately to West Freugh from where they flew to London for meetings with the War Cabinet before continuing their journey to Moscow. Their journey was completed aboard Catalina W8416 of 210 Squadron based at Oban which picked them up at Invergordon on 18 September for a 17½ hour flight round Norway's North Cape to Archangel where they arrived at 0740 on 19 September to transfer to a Russian aircraft which flew them to Moscow for talks with Joseph Stalin and his military leaders. On 21 September they joined Catalina W8414 of 210 Squadron at Archangel for the return journey to Invergordon.

On 18 April 1942 a Pan American Airways Boeing Clipper "Modicum" which had arrived on 16 April left Stranraer for the United States via Newfoundland carrying the Chief of Naval Staff, Admiral Sir Dudley Pound, General Marshall, US Chief of Army Staff (who later initiated the Marshall Plan for aid to post-war Europe) and Harry Hopkins who was Franklin Roosevelt's personal assistant throughout the war years.

On 16 June 1942 British Overseas Airways Corporation Boeing Clipper G-AGDZ "Bristol" with a crew of fourteen commanded by Captain Kelly-Rogers arrived at Stranraer from Foynes on the Shannon Estuary where BOAC and Pan American Airways had established a war-time transatlantic flying boat terminal. 'Bristol' was one of three Boeing Clippers which BOAC had purchased from Pan American Airways in May 1941 at a cost of £260,000 each. All three aircraft were used on cross-Atlantic services, initially from Foynes to Baltimore then from mid 1945,

Poole to Baltimore. The following night at 11.30 pm "Bristol" left Stranraer for Newfoundland carrying a party who had arrived from London aboard a special train. The party comprised Prime Minister Winston Churchill, his Principal Private Secretary John Martin, his ADC Lieutenant Commander C R Thompson and his doctor, Sir Charles Wilson. Military members were General Sir Alan Brooke, Major General Sir Hastings Ismay and Brigadier D G Stewart.

After a brief stop in Newfoundland to refuel, "Bristol" landed on the Potomac River in Washington on 18 June. After meetings with President Roosevelt the party returned aboard "Bristol" leaving Baltimore on 25 June. Refuelling in Newfoundland en route, Stranraer was reached at 5 am on 27 June. The Prime Minister and his party left immediately aboard a special train which arrived at Euston station at 5 pm to be met by Mrs Churchill and several members of the War Cabinet.

General Brooke later noted in his diary "a huge flying boat beautifully fitted with sleeping bunks, dining saloon, steward's office etc".

An unusual visitor to Stranraer from 30 May to 3 June and again from 14 July to 15 August 1942 was a Heinkel He115 twin engined seaplane, a type used by the Luftwaffe for maritime reconnaissance. When it arrived on the second visit it was escorted by a Norwegian Air Force Lockheed Hudson which suggests that this was one of the six He115s purchased by Norway just before the war. When Norway fell to invading German forces in June 1940 four He115s were flown out by their Norwegian crews to the RAF flying boat base at Sullom Voe in the Shetlands. Within weeks of their arrival these aircraft were placed under the direct control of the Air Ministry Inteligence Branch. Based at Calshot on the Solent they were modified to be used on covert operations which largely involved delivery and pick-up of secret agents on enemy coastlines.

Early in 1942 a Canadian Flight Lieutenant who had been Squadron Navigation Officer with 240 Squadron when they were based in Stranraer volunteered for an "interesting job". He was posted to Calshot where he was to spend nine months flying with a

24. Heinkel He115 Seaplane in RAF livery   *IWM E(Mos)1230*

Norwegian pilot in an He115 making frequent night flights to remote spots on the Bay of Biscay coastline.

In May 1942 returning from such an operation at first light they were attacked just off the Isle of Wight by an RAF Spitfire. Despite having one propellor shot off and a wing on fire they managed to land safely, extinguish the fire then radio for help. They were soon reached by an air sea rescue launch which towed them back to Calshot. A subsequent court of enquiry established that due to a breakdown in intelligence communication two pilots from a Polish Spitfire Squadron who had taken off to patrol around the Isle of Wight had not been advised that they might encounter a "friendly" He115.

The He115 which visited Stranraer was there to train new crew members this being considered an ideal base from which to practice, for example, night landings in unlit coastal inlets.

When 4 (C) OTU finally severed its connections with Stranraer in November 1942 302 Ferry Training Unit moved from Killadeas, Lough Erne to Stranraer on 1 December 1942. Little remains on record about this Unit except that it was equipped with Catalina and Sunderland aircraft on which crews were trained for "ferry" or delivery flights, presumably cross-Atlantic or to flying boat squadrons serving overseas.

On 30 April 1942 the station was visited by HRH The Duchess of Gloucester who, as Air Chief Commandant, inspected WAAF personnel.

When in July 1943 302 Ferry Training Unit transferred to Oban RAF Station Stranraer was left without a resident unit. From 27 July the Station was placed on a care and maintenance basis whilst personnel were transferred elsewhere, the final batch to RAF Station Castle Kennedy on 1 September 1943. Launches, moorings and other remaining equipment was taken over by 57 Maintenance Unit, Wig Bay. In November a number of requisitioned buildings in Stranraer were returned to their owners before the Station was finally disbanded on 15 February 1944.

CHAPTER 8

57 MAINTENANCE UNIT, WIG BAY

Loch Ryan as has been noted was first used by RAF flying boats in 1929. Some of the first moorings laid then were in the shelter of the sand spit forming Wig Bay close to Kirkcolm village on the west side of Loch Ryan some five miles north of Stranraer. The first suggestion of a permanent flying boat base being established here came in August 1937 when unconfirmed reports suggested that a Stranraer flying boat of 228 Squadron which visited Wig Bay for three days, carried senior officers who were assessing the viability of the location. Eighteen months later the local press reported on 28 January 1939 that Air Ministry officials "have again paid visits to the Kirkcolm district giving rise to the belief that plans for an air base are imminent". The first officially recorded indication came in November 1940 when an Air Ministry team visited RAF Station Stranraer to carry out surveys at Wig Bay. Nothing further is recorded until 12 March 1942 when 1 Flying Boat Servicing Unit was set up at Wig Bay. Their task initially was to ease pressure on operational Stations by undertaking major overhauls on Sunderlands from 201 and 228 Squadrons. As this concept developed they were joined on 15 July 1943 by 11 Flying Boat Fitting Unit. On 16 August sixteen Sunderlands from 201, 220, 228, 422 and 461 Squadrons were undergoing overhaul and twenty-eight fully serviceable Sunderlands were held in reserve.

On 8 October 1943 57 Maintenance Unit was formed at Wig Bay absorbing the two Fitting and Servicing Units. The purpose of 57 MU was defined as preparation, modification, repair and storage of Consolidated Catalina, Martin Mariner and Short Sunderland flying boats. By July 1944 two hangars had been built and twenty-six hardstandings were in use at Scar Point. Supermarine Walrus, Fairey Sea Otter and Consolidated Coronado were added to the types of aircraft handled. When the unit opened accommodation was available for 1520 Officers and men and for 220 airwomen.

Catalinas were first supplied to the RAF under Lease-Lend arrangements from early in 1941. The first one to arrive flew into Scottish Aviation Ltd's flying boat base at Greenock on the Clyde on 1 February 1941. Thereafter until November 1944 Scottish Aviation at Greenock, then from 1943, Largs received all lease-lend Catalinas and other flying boats arriving cross-Atlantic. Flying boats arriving at Largs were moored on the leeward side of Great Cumbrae Island to be converted to RAF requirements - armament, radar, wireless, etc, by Scottish Aviation. In November 1944 responsibility for Catalina conversion passsed to 57 MU which had for over twelve months been maintaining and overhauling Catalinas for the ten operational squadrons with which they flew.

Also handled were ten Consolidated Coronados which had been supplied to the RAF in 1943 under lease-lend agreements. An all metal monoplane with four Pratt & Whitney Twin Wasp engines, all ten were flown by 231 Squadron, Transport Command. Other US built flying boats handled were the twenty Martin Mariners, also supplied under lease-lend, which were flown by 524 Squadron, Coastal Command, based at Oban. The Mariner had two 1700 hp Wright Cyclone engines giving a range of 3,200 miles.

A Mariner which developed an electrical fault whilst taxying at Wig Bay on 3 November 1944 was completely destroyed by fire.

On 14 December 1944 the first direct transatlantic delivery of Catalinas from the US was made. Unfortunately the three Catalinas arrived in SE gale conditions and could not be diverted as they were short of fuel. One, out of fuel, force-landed in the open sea off Ballantrae; the crew were brought ashore by launch whilst the plane was eventually towed in on 27 December after two weeks lying at anchor just off Girvan to where it had been towed for shelter. The other two planes landed at Wig Bay in conditions so severe that one was blown ashore with damage which necessitated write-off.

By January 1945 the Unit personnel numbered over one thousand and the number of aircraft held was one hundred and seventy, many of which were Sunderland III being converted to Sunderland V standard.

A major part of the conversion involved replacing the 1065 hp Bristol Pegasus engines with 1200 hp Pratt and Whitney Twin Wasp engines. The early Sunderland models were equipped with 965 hp Bristol Pegasus engines with fixed-pitch propellors which in the not uncommon event of an engine failure could not be feathered. To prevent windmilling with the consequent difficulties for the pilot it became practice when an engine failed to land on the sea, if this was possible the crew would then tie the propellor with rope to the engine stay, then take off on three engines. Over 50 Sunderlands were re-fitted with Pratt and Whitney engines at 57 MU between mid 1944 and the end of the war. The first to be converted was test flown, fully laden, by the Unit Senior Test Pilot, a Squadron Leader, who surprised onlookers by flying over Wig Bay first on two engines, then for a few moments on one engine which would have been impossible with Pegasus engines.

In 1945 a Sunderland Mark V based at Pembroke Dock flew a routine anti-submarine patrol over the Bay of Biscay which was uneventful until in unexpected severe weather they flew into a cumulo nimbus cloud and promptly involuntarily looped the loop. Aircraft and crew were unharmed and returned safely to Pembroke Dock where the Engineering Officer decided to have the aircraft flown to 57 MU for a complete overhaul. Nothing was found to be amiss but to be quite certain the Sunderland was towed by a pinnace to Short Brothers factory at Belfast where another full check found nothing wrong.

With the end of the war in Europe in May 1945, pressure did not ease as 57 MU was given the additional task of storage, pending disposal, of large numbers of surplus to requirement land planes. On 21 June 1945 the airfields at West Freugh and Castle Kennedy became Sub-Storage Units, the first until July 1947 and the latter until November 1946. De Havilland Mosquitoes were stored in large numbers; for example eighty-three were held at West Freugh and forty-five at Castle Kennedy at the end of February 1946. A number were prepared for delivery to Belgian, French and Turkish Air Forces; most were sold as scrap after removal of armament, radar etc.

25. Aerial view of flying boats awaiting disposal at Wig Bay   A. Thompson

Meantime large numbers of flying boats were also becoming surplus; storage at Wig Bay reached a peak of one hundred and eighty-three in July 1945. As with the land planes some were prepared for further use; for example a few Sunderlands were "demilitarised" for use as civil transport planes. In December 1945 nine Catalinas were despatched to the Norwegian Air Force; then in July 1946 eighteen Catalinas were prepared for sale to Brazil and four Sunderlands for sale to South Africa, followed in August by five Sunderlands for sale to Turkey.

Some older Catalinas and Sunderlands were disposed of by sinking them in the North Channel after removing engines, armament, radar, etc. Twenty two Sunderlands were towed out individually to a point some two miles north of Milleur Point towards Ailsa Craig. Floats were literally ripped off by attaching a rope to the towing pinnace, then their pinnace crew holed the hull in several places with judicious axe blows.

One of the types which passed through was the Short Seaford, a development of the Sunderland IV. Eight Seafords were built during 1945, four of which were held at Wig Bay in December 1946 after having been on trial with 201 Squadron. In October 1947 six Seafords were taken over by the Ministry of Civil Aviation to be converted to Solent 3 civil flying boats for BOAC. In March 1947 forty-two Sunderlands and sixty-one Catalinas were sold to Phoenix Iron Works as scrap, followed in October 1947 by a further twenty Catalinas and ten Sunderlands.

By the end of 1948 most of the "scrap" planes had been disposed of and the Unit personnel had fallen to five hundred. The task was now preparation and storage of Sunderlands for RAF Squadrons; from January 1950 six were prepared each month, three for Coastal Command and three for Far East Air Force. A small number of Sunderlands were also being prepared for despatch to the Royal New Zealand Air Force.

In July 1951 the Air Ministry decided to contract all Sunderland maintenance to Short & Harland Ltd who took over the Wig Bay complex in September 1951. The only RAF personnel remaining were those of the Flying Boat Test Unit who, in addition to test flying, monitored Sunderland preparation by the civilian

Contractor. In June 1954 a RNZAF crew flew into West Freugh to take delivery of the last of the sixteen Sunderlands which had been prepared for the RNZAF. Finally the Test Unit was transferred to Pembroke Dock on 1 November 1955 thus severing the RAF connection with Loch Ryan which had commenced in 1928, though two tenuous links do still exist. One is a Stranraer flying boat, believed to be the only biplane flying boat still in existence, which is on display in the Royal Air Force Museum, Hendon. The other link is a Sandringham civil flying boat, a direct Sunderland derivative, which was at the end of 1990 the only remaining member of a long line of Sunderland type flying boats still in flying condition. She has an interesting history.

Built in Belfast in 1944 as Sunderland MkIII, ML 814, she joined 201 Squadron for operational service in March 1944 and also flew with 422 Squadron before returning to Belfast early in 1945 for conversion to MkV standards. She then saw service with 330 Squadron before being sent to 57 Maintenance Unit in November 1946, remaining in storage at Wig Bay until sold to the Royal New Zealand Air Force in 1953.

In New Zealand as NZ 4108 she flew for ten years between the mainland and the many island dependencies of New Zealand in the Pacific Ocean.

In 1963 NZ4108 was sold to Ansett Airways in Australia who carried out a major rebuild to Short Sandringham civil flying boat standard. She then went into service as VH BRF "Islander" to provide a regular scheduled service to Lord Howe Island which lies off the Australian Pacific coast. In 1974 VH BRF was sold to Antilles Air Boats, based in the United States Virgin Islands, who renamed her "Excalibur VIII". A short time later she was laid up in nearby Puerto Rico.

Five years later in June 1979 she was purchased in a near derelict state by Sir Edward Hulton. After extensive repair she was flown to Marseilles in March 1981 for further overhaul. Eventually registered in Great Britain as G-BJHS before being flown to London, she landed in the Thames in August 1982. She remained in the Pool of London for several months before being flown to Southampton Water to be beached close to the former RAF Flying

Boat Station at Calshot Spit for yet more maintenance and overhaul. In 1984 she was flown to the Medway to be moored alongside Short Brothers' factory at Rochester and remained there until towed downstream to the former Royal Naval Dockyard at Chatham where covered accommodation was available for the work still being carried out by Short Brothers.

On 16 October 1987 the now 43-year-old flying boat was damaged by the hurricane force winds which swept over southern England. The prospect of yet more costly repairs forced Sir Edward Hulton, who had already invested millions of pounds endeavouring to keep her in flying condition, to offer her for sale. There followed a lease for a short period to Ryanair, an Irish charter company with a base at Foynes on the Shannon estuary. In their livery she made several airshow appearances during 1989. About this time she was the subject of a short documentary film which was shown on television by Channel 4 early in 1990.

When the Ryanair lease ended she returned to Southampton Water whilst efforts continued to find a buyer. Her final public appearance in Great Britain came when she spent the first two weeks of July 1990 moored near Bowness on Lake Windermere close to where Short Brothers had established a Sunderland production line during the war years. Eventually on 19 July 1993 she took off from Calshot to fly via Foynes, Iceland and Newfoundland to her new owner in Florida.

CHAPTER 9

RDF STATION NORTH CAIRN

Largely due to the efforts of Robert Watson Watt in developing Radio Direction Finding - as Radar was then known - we had on the outbreak of war in 1939 a system greatly more advanced than the German system which had also been in the process of development for several years.

An Air Ministry meeting held in May 1939 discussed the advisability of providing Radio Direction Finding cover for the cities in Britain which were considered likely to become the target of enemy raids. In further discussion one of the cities looked at was Belfast which it was agreed could best be protected by an RDF station located in the vicinity of Stranraer. By November 1939 a site had been selected for this station at Mid Moile on high ground to the north of Cairnryan close to the County boundary with Ayrshire. However, this site was not proceeded with mainly because of the expected difficulty in constructing an approach road in rough moorland country. An alternative site on the coastline at North Cairn Farm a few miles north of Portpatrick was selected instead.

By early 1941 more than 50 RDF stations were operating in Great Britain, most of them on the east coast. In April 1941 construction work at North Cairn, including the erection of two 360 foot towers and several lower towers was complete allowing Air Ministry Experimental Station No. 60 to become CHL Station No. 54, one of the few operational west coast stations.

At this time the equipment at North Cairn could detect aircraft flying at heights of over 500 feet within a distance of 25 miles. No record is available but it is certain that enemy aircraft heading for Northern Ireland were detected from time to time though not in large numbers. It is likely that Focke Wulf Condors flying over the North Channel from their bases in Norway were sometimes detected. Probably the largest number of enemy aircraft detected at any one time were those taking part in the Clydeside Blitz, particularly attacks on Clydebank which took place in the first few weeks after North Cairn became operational. These aircraft were guided to their targets by following a radio beam system which German technicians had perfected during raids on Coventry and other cities in England. The beam, several kilometres wide, would have led north from the Irish Sea to Clydebank with the western edge passing within a few miles of and well within range of the North Cairn transmitter.

Accommodation on the station, as with others rapidly built with limited wartime resources, was somewhat spartan, however airmen and airwomen, as they always did, contrived to make themselves reasonably comfortable using their ingenuity to make unauthorised furniture etc. from odds and ends scrounged from every available source.

One airman who served at North Cairn was Aircraftsman (Second Class) Anthony Hancock. In his biography 'Tony Hancock - Artiste' published in 1978 Roger Wilmut writes 'In 1942 Hancock volunteered for the RAF. After initial training he was transferred to Stranraer where as an AC 2 (General Duties) he was placed in charge of the coal dump.' The unit to which he had been posted was North Cairn where a fellow airman described him as 'a shuffling fellow with a sad face and with heavy lidded eyes.' When in 1943 it was suggested that North Cairn 'inmates' should set up their own Concert Party because they had so little officially organised entertainment Hancock responded enthusiastically. He readily agreed to take part and also contributed several sketches which he had written which were very well received when the first show was given in the recreation building. Encouraged by his success Hancock applied for transfer to one of the 'Gang Shows' run by Squadron Leader Ralph Reader to provide entertainment for servicemen. Though his application was not successful he was not deterred and made two further applications - each requiring an interview in London which gave a welcome three day break from his North Cairn duties - before he was eventually accepted. He was posted to Gang Show Number Nine and before long was touring with this troupe in Southern Italy and Greece.

As the war drew to an end the services of a Chain Home Low station on the west coast were not considered to be of major consequence and North Cairn station was placed on a care and maintenance basis early in March 1945.

CHAPTER 10

MARINE CRAFT TRAINING SCHOOL, CORSEWALL

The first marine launches used by the RAF in the early days of flying boat operations were based on Admiralty designs. These launches were ideal for routine duties but were not fast enough when required for the rescue work which inevitably arose when accidents involving flying boats occurred. In 1930 the RAF commissioned the design and construction of faster launches to be used specifically for rescue duties thus laying the foundations of what was to become, some ten years later, a large Air Sea Rescue organisation. Many of the initial series of tests on a 37-foot, 200 hp craft with a speed of 23 knots, were undertaken at the Flying Boat Station at Cattewater, Plymouth. One of the airmen actively involved was Aircraftman Shaw - better known as Lieutenant Colonel T E Lawrence or Lawrence of Arabia.

With increasing numbers of marine craft coming into use the Air Ministry established a Marine Training School at Calshot on Southampton Water in 1927. This school, which expanded rapidly after the outbreak of war in 1939, remained at Calshot until repeated enemy air raids in the Solent area made their position untenable; thus on 1 August 1942 the School transferred to Corsewall on the west shore of Loch Ryan eight miles north of Stranraer, as 1 Marine Craft Training School, RAF Station, Corsewall.

The prime duty of the School was to train marine crews with the additional task of supplying all craft required by nearby 57 Maintenance Unit, Wig Bay. The School was fortunate to take over a ready-made camp of sixty-five buildings which had been erected to house a US Flying Boat Unit which was to have operated from Loch Ryan until, apparently, policy decisions decreed otherwise. Construction of this camp had commenced following decisions reached at a conference in Washington in January 1941 when it was agreed that if the United States should enter the war, two US Navy flying boat bases would be required in Great Britain, one in Loch Ryan and one in Lough Erne. Corsewall House was taken over as Station Headquarters.

All personnel engaged in Air Sea Rescue and other marine craft duties had to pass through the Marine Training School; indeed many airmen who completed basic training courses returned to Corsewall later in their service for further training.

The basic training course for motor boat crew lasted for three months. The first practical lessons were on how to row a small boat; when this was accomplished each trainee had to scull the boat, using only one oar, along a straight line course. Only after passing rowing and sculling tests were trainees allowed to progress to training on powered dinghies and marine tenders; they also learned how to handle boat hooks, heaving lines, fenders and moorings, frequently in cold, wet conditions. Except in very severe weather half of each day was spent at sea and half in the classroom.

In addition to motor boat crew other training courses covered all aspects of marine craft operation including Marine Craft Officers: - 1st Class Coxswain - a Flight Sergeant or Sergeant: 2nd Class Coxswain - generally a Corporal: Marine Fitter: Carpenter/Boat Builder: Astro Navigation.

An Air Sea Rescue launch crew normally consisted of an officer as Skipper with 1st and 2nd coxswains, two or three deckhands, one medical orderly, one wireless operator and two marine engineers, one of whom would be a senior NCO.

The craft used at Corsewall ranged from twelve-foot dinghies through whalers, tenders including fire tenders, pinnaces, bomb scows and refuelling tankers to a 115-foot "D Class" long range rescue craft which joined the School in January 1946. With four 1250 hp Packard Merlin engines this vessel had a maximum speed of 33 knots. The bulk of training was carried out on 60-foot general service pinnaces which had three 130 hp Perkins diesel engines and in 42-foot seaplane tenders of pre-war design which had two Perkins diesel engines; over four hundred of these tenders were used by the RAF, forty of them as fire tenders.

Most high speed launch training was on the 68-foot "Type 3" launch which had three 500 hp Napier Sea Lion engines, an adaptation of the Napier Lion aero engine, giving a speed of 28 knots.

All pinnaces and high speed launches were armed; most had two or three Boulton Paul aircraft type gun turrets each with two Browning .303 machine guns whilst some also had a 20 mm Oerlikon cannon mounted aft. All trainees passing through the School were given gunnery training. When at peak strength the School had a staff of seven hundred with up to two hundred and seventy-five trainees spending two thousand hours a month at sea on training and six hundred hours a month on duty with 57 MU Wig Bay. Several obsolete or unserviceable flying boats were used for beaching, launching, towing and handling exercises. Navigation exercises involving reasonably long periods in the open sea eg to Peel, Isle of Man, to Larne and to Belfast were undertaken regularly without regard to weather conditions. As a contribution to fresh food supplies airmen cultivated six acres of ground within the camp boundaries in their free time producing potatoes and other vegetables for the School kitchens. Visitors to the School included Brigadier Bruce White, Royal Engineers, who had overall responsibility for the construction of No 2 Military Port on the other side of Loch Ryan, who visited on 14 February 1943; then on 26 February Lieutenant Commander Bryce, Senior Naval Officer, Stranraer, visited. Close liaison was essential in the busy waters of Loch Ryan. On 30 March 1943 WAAF personnel were inspected by HRH The Duchess of Gloucester, Air Commandant in Chief.

In addition to training, launches from the School were occasionally involved in other duties. On 3 February 1943 Pinnaces 99 and 478 rescued the crew of a Blackburn Botha which had ditched off Ailsa Craig. Literally moments later the plane sank. On 3 November 1944 Fire Tender 34 was called to Wig Bay where a Martin Mariner flying boat was on fire but was unable to prevent the Mariner being burned out. On 14 December 1944 Pinnace 82 attended a Consolidated Catalina which had force landed off Ballantrae in severe weather when heading for 57 Maintenance Unit, Wig Bay. When the weather abated the Catalina was towed to a sheltered anchorage at the entrance to Girvan Harbour where it remained until Pinnace 33 towed it to Wig Bay on 27 December.

A launch from the School became involved in a more serious incident on 16 January 1945 when High Speed Launch 2734 left Corsewall at 2.30 pm for trials following an engine refit. At 3.20 pm a coded "Vessel in Distress" signal was received giving a location some miles off Ballantrae. Changing course they soon sighted a Royal Navy aircraft carrier escorting a Tanker. They were advised that the tanker had been torpedoed and had on board eight dead and three injured seamen. At 4.25 pm HSL 2734 took on board the injured men, landing them one hour later at Wig Bay where medical assistance was waiting. The three seamen were taken by ambulance to the RAF Hospital, Lochnaw where one was found to be dead on arrival. A message of thanks was later received from the Senior Naval Officer, Clyde Area.

With the end of the war in May 1945, numbers in training reduced though the School remained active; in January 1946 seven different Trade Courses were in hand. In August 1946, though 57 MU was less active than during the war, two hundred and seventy-five hours were spent at sea on MU duty. In October 1946 the School was advised that it was to move to Felixstowe, a move which was completed by 31 December 1946.

CHAPTER 11

64 AIR SEA RESCUE UNIT AND 1106 MARINE CRAFT UNIT, DRUMMORE

When 4 Armament Training Unit, West Freugh opened in January 1937 two bombing targets were erected at the head of Luce Bay. It was necessary to have launches to service these targets and to provide safety cover when bombing practice was in progress. Three launches under the control of the West Freugh Unit were based in the harbour at Drummore, which is the most southerly village in Scotland, from April 1937. They were joined soon after by two Armoured Target Boats. It is believed these boats were used to tow floating targets used for air to sea gunnery practice. The armour was to protect the crew against the risk of erratic aim by a trainee gunner firing his single Vickers Gas Operated machine gun from the under-belly turret of a Handley Page Heyford!

During May 1942 64 Air Sea Rescue Unit was formed at Drummore. In addition to range safety duties the Unit operated two Air Sea Rescue launches. During the following two-and-a-half years frequent searches for crashed aircraft in the Luce Bay and North Channel area were undertaken though rarely with success. Several bodies were recovered and once, on 19 November 1943, the crew of a ditched Avro Anson was picked up uninjured off Port Logan.

Regular assistance was given to the Bombing Trials Unit, West Freugh, inspecting targets in Luce Bay and taking observers to sea to view bombing trials. On 1 September 1944 64 Air Sea Rescue Unit was transferred to Ayr where it remained until disbanded in February 1946.

After a gap of several years 1106 Marine Craft Unit was formed at Drummore on 2 January 1952 with the Bombing Trials

Unit, West Freugh as parent unit. The Unit with a Warrant Officer in charge of twenty-five airmen operated three marine tenders and two dinghies to provide safety boats for Luce Bay ranges. During the next six and a half years a variety of tasks was undertaken at the behest of the Bombing Trials Unit. From June 1952 a drifter moored in Luce Bay as a "very high level" bombing target was visited regularly to be inspected and to be pumped out. During 1953 and 1954 there were several references to work in connection with anti-submarine bombing exercises. In March 1954 there were specific references to visits to a target in use by the Bombing Trials Unit to test 10,000 lb bombs. The range was always patrolled when in use to ensure safety, fishing boats being "warned off" from time to time.

1106 Marine Craft Unit ceased to operate in mid-1959 when the Bombing Trials Unit became part of the Royal Aircraft Establishment.

Two Ministry of Defence Range patrol vessels, the Aquila Maris, based at Portpatrick and a launch numbered LI380 based at Drummore were in use until 1998 when both were withdrawn. Maritime support when required is now provided by the West Freugh contractor using chartered vessels. Drummore harbour is used to maintain floating targets and to moor them when not in use. When visited in Spring 2000 two brightly coloured targets were held in the harbour together with two or three badly damaged and apparently abandoned older targets. It was noted that the buildings erected in 1942 to accommodate the original Air Sea Rescue Unit remain at the harbourside apparently in good repair and in use as a garage by a haulage company.

CHAPTER 12

11 SATELLITE LANDING GROUND, LOW ELDRIG

In December 1940 18 Maintenance Unit, Dumfries was engaged in servicing and preparing aircraft for issue as required to airfields around Great Britain. Due to the large turnover of aircraft additional storage space was required particularly as dispersal of aircraft was considered to be a useful safety measure. Accordingly 18 MU acquired three Satellite Landing Grounds of which one, designated as 11 Satellite Landing Ground, was situated at Low Eldrig some four-and-a-half miles north of Drummore on a stretch of level grassland about 1250 yards long running parallel to the road between Ardwell and Drummore.

After an inspection on 7 December 1940 it was decided to prepare the site by clearing and rolling a grass landing strip. A further inspection in May 1941 found the strip to have areas of peat, making it very soft in wet weather. The first aircraft to use the strip was a De Havilland Dominie from 18 MU which made several trial landings and take-offs on 3 June 1941. It was decided that the strip could be used only in fine weather by small aircraft.

The first aircraft to be dispersed were four Fairey Battles which landed on 29 June. A Hawker Hurricane which landed on 27 July hit a soft patch causing it to completely turn over, with consequent damage to the propellor and undercarriage. On 14 August the Officer Commanding 18 MU visited by road. He drove his car down the airstrip only to have it bog down at the southern end! All aircraft were flown out before the end of October.

Over the next few months contractors excavated a lot of peat and drainage was installed; however the strip remained unusable until May 1942. From May until September up to twenty-five aircraft at a time, mostly Battles and Blenheims were stored with frequent movements in and out. When the strip was in use the aircraft were guarded by a detachment of Royal Scots Fusiliers from their base in Stranraer.

The last seven aircraft were flown out on 30 September 1942 with no further use being made of 11 Satellite Landing Ground.

CHAPTER 13

RAF HOSPITAL, LOCHNAW

In mid-1940, with an increasing number of service men and women being based in and around Stranraer, Lochnaw Castle five miles north west of Stranraer was taken over for use as an Auxiliary Hospital. Early in 1942 when it was proposed to install a United States Navy flying boat base in Loch Ryan, the use of this hospital was offered to the US Navy who declined, preferring to build a hospital to their own specification in the grounds of Lochnaw Castle.

In June 1942 the hospital in the Castle was offered instead to the RAF who, with some eight thousand personnel based within ten miles of Stranraer, readily accepted. RAF Hospital, Lochnaw with three RAF doctors and nursing staff from Princess Mary's RAF Nursing Service came into use on 1 July 1942.

The RAF Nursing Service was formed in 1918 shortly after the RAF was founded. In 1923 when Princess Mary, the future Princess Royal, became patron the name was changed to Princess Mary's RAF Nursing Service. The Princess had a life-long interest in nursing having, after a nursing training course, worked in Great Ormond Street Children's Hospital during World War I. In World War II in addition to her nursing interests she was also Controller Commandant of the Auxiliary Territorial Service.

Shortly afterwards the US Navy abandoned their intent to move into Loch Ryan leaving their half-built hospital unrequired. The RAF agreed to take over the project on 25 August. Progress to complete the new buildings was slow largely due to the US specification which meant that equipment was difficult to obtain. For example a water chlorination plant could not be commissioned due to lack of US-designed parts. Further problems arose on 24 November 1942 when two wards in the new building were destroyed by fire. It was 15 March 1943 before the first twenty-eight beds in

the new buildings could be brought into use. On 25 May the "old" hospital in the Castle was closed down with one hundred and one beds in use in the new buildings.

Early in June 1943 with one hundred and eleven beds and three operating theatres in use the hospital was commanded by a Wing Commander Doctor assisted by one Squadron Leader Surgeon, one Squadron Leader Physician and one female Flight Lieutenant Doctor. Nursing staff were led by a Matron with seven Nursing Sisters. Regular visits were paid by specialists from other RAF hospitals, eg Neurologist, Opthalmist, Psychiatrist and Gynaecologist.

On 23 April 1944 HRH The Princess Royal accompanied by Air Marshall Sir Harold Wittingham, Director General of RAF Medical Services and The Matron in Chief visited to inspect the hospital; arriving at 2 pm they left at 5 pm after having tea in the Sisters' Mess.

In June 1944 the hospital finally reached full potential with sixteen wards, each with ten beds, in use. On 15 January 1945 two injured and one "dead on arrival" Norwegian merchant seamen were admitted after being brought ashore from a torpedoed merchant ship in a launch from nearby Corsewall Marine Craft Training School. After treatment the injured men together with their deceased colleague were taken to Glasgow in the care of the Norwegian Consul.

Since inception in July 1942 the hospital had dealt with the full range of illness and injury including injuries from an occasional flying accident. When the war in Europe ended the hospital began to receive patients returning to Great Britain from overseas. During June, July and August 1945 eight batches of from twelve to twenty patients were received directly from hospital ships arriving in Liverpool from the Middle East and India; then in September three patients arrived who had been flown home from Singapore.

During September the hospital was advised to prepare for closure on 31 October 1945. Remaining patients were dispersed to other hospitals and staff transferred. A quantity of equipment which included one complete operating theatre went to West Freugh where the West of Scotland RAF Hospital was based from November 1945 until closure on 30 November 1949.

CHAPTER 14

RAF STATION, CASTLE KENNEDY

On 6 June 1941 an advance party from Central Gunnery School, Warmwell, Dorset arrived at West Freugh to take over a grass strip airfield at Cults Farm, Castle Kennedy, three-and-a-half miles south east of Stranraer. The grass strips to be used were virtually the same as those used by 2 Squadron, Royal Flying Corps when they spent a short time here in August and September 1913. This same location had been used when Alan Cobham's Air Circus visited for four days commencing 29 June 1933. Aircraft taking part included an Avro 504K, an Airspeed Ferry three engined biplane, De Havilland Gipsy Moth and Tiger Moth biplanes together with a Cierva Autogiro in which members of the public could purchase a seven minute flight for five shillings (25p).

By the end of June the transfer of Central Gunnery School was complete with Bristol Blenheim, Handley Page Hampden and Vickers Wellington aircraft ready to commence No 19 Gunnery Leader Course on 3 July.

On 28 July 10 Air Gunnery School was formed at Castle Kennedy, their first training course commencing on 17 August with thirty-five trainee Gunners who were flown in Boulton Paul Defiants, the only RAF single engined aircraft to be fitted with a power operated gun turret. The Blackburn Roc, another single engined aircraft fitted with a Boulton Paul turret, flew only with the Fleet Air Arm. The Defiant which had a 1260 hp Rolls Royce Merlin engine played a small role in the Battle of Britain where the lack of forward firing guns left it at some disadvantage when under attack by enemy fighters. It was used by Air Gunnery Schools for only a few months before being switched to target tug duties for which the gun turret was removed. Two hundred and ninety target tug versions were built for use by Gunnery Schools and Anti Aircraft

Co-operation Units. Whilst Defiants were being used by gunnery trainees target towing Lysanders were used for air to air gunnery training over the North Channel and Firth of Clyde.

From early in August until mid October due to persistent rainfall the airfield was waterlogged requiring all flying by Central Gunnery School and 10 AGS to be from nearby West Freugh airfield. During this period Castle Kennedy was used for accommodation only; some discomfort must have been borne by the one hundred and forty airmen who were housed under canvas from August until 28 October when they were rehoused in Dunragit House some three miles from Castle Kennedy. During October four Supermarine Spitfires from 122 Squadron were attached to Central Gunnery School for tactical exercises.

Early in December Central Gunnery School moved to Chelveston, Northants, then on 18 December 10 AGS moved to Walney Island, Barrow-in-Furness. This allowed the airfield to be closed down for the construction of two concrete runways, both 1400 yards long by 50 yards wide. Four Callender-Hamilton hangars and nine Blister hangars were also erected at this time and accommodation extended to house one thousand six hundred men and two hundred and eighty women. After four months the airfield re-opened on 13 April 1942 when 3 Air Gunnery School was formed, equipped with Blackburn Bothas and target towing Fairey Battles. Number One Training Course was completed on 5 May when forty-nine Air Gunners qualified. On 28 May ten Australian and forty-two Canadian Sergeant Air Gunners who had qualified in their home countries arrived for a refresher course. On 13 June twelve Polish pilots arrived to join the School as staff pilots. Training courses were now commencing at two week intervals; on 12 August 1942 four concurrent courses were running with sixty trainees each. The aircraft complement was now forty-six Bothas and twenty-seven Battles.

Marshall of the Royal Air Force, Lord Trenchard, visited Castle Kennedy on 26 August making one of his periodic "Inspector General" tours. Unfortunately on the day of his visit a Battle and a Botha collided in mid air with several serious casualties.

26. Roll of achievement, IV Bombing & Gunnery School, West Freugh *TEE*

In September Battles began to be replaced by the Miles Martinet which was the first RAF aircraft to have been designed as a target tug. A start was also being made to replace Bothas with Avro Ansons fitted with power operated gun turrets. By the end of November forty-seven Ansons had totally replaced Bothas. Total flying hours in November were nine hundred and eighty-five.

During the first two weeks of December 1942 3 AGS was transferred to Mona, Anglesey taking with them sixty aircraft. The AGS was immediately replaced by 2 Torpedo Training Unit which was formed at Castle Kennedy on 19 December 1942 equipped with twelve Bristol Beauforts. Coastal Command aircrews were trained in the art of torpedo dropping in an area of the Firth of Clyde south of Arran. In order to release a torpedo with an accurate trajectory it was necessary to fly a straight and level course towards the target at a height of exactly 72 feet over the sea at an airspeed of 70 knots. Inaccurate height and speed would cause the torpedo to enter the water at the wrong angle and probably break up. Apart from possibly allowing the target to escape a live torpedo cost around £2000.

The Senior Naval Officer Clyde Area co-operated with the Unit by making available a Destroyer for training exercises when he was so requested. Beauforts and Beaufighters could then make mock attacks whilst on board cameras filmed the ship and later also the pilot's instrument panel for later assesment of the attack by course instructors. These exercises also provided valuable anti-aircraft practice for the destroyer crew.

In February 1943 Bristol Beaufighters adapted for torpedo dropping were added to the strength. Courses normally lasted four weeks with twenty-five crews on each course.

Between 23 March and 11 September 1943 three fatal flying accidents involving Beaufighters were recorded with five deaths. On 29 September 1943 2 Torpedo Training Unit was transferred to Turnberry where it was absorbed by 1 Torpedo Training Unit already based there.

Towards the end of October 1943 3 Air Gunnery School returned to Castle Kennedy from Mona bringing with them twenty-three Ansons and twenty-five Martinets. Gunnery training continued

on the same basis as formerly. One training course commencing
on 6 November included twenty-three French trainees. In April
1944 the Station had a personnel strength of one thousand one
hundred and thirty-eight of whom two hundred and thirty-seven
were trainees. In June and July 1944 there were two fatal accidents
involving two 3 AGS planes, an Anson and a Martinet which crashed
causing seven deaths.

Unusual visitors for four weeks from 21 November were six
Supermarine Spitfires from 17 Service Flying Training School, the
flying school attached to the RAF College at Cranwell. 17 SFTS
records show the detachment as being 5 Turkish Advanced Air
Firing Course. 3 AGS records list four accidents involving Spitfires
with Turkish pilots - on 27 November a Spitfire ground looped on
landing, on 1 December and again on 12 December Spitfires had
their undercarriages damaged by heavy landings, and on 19
December a Spitfire hit a stationary Anson whilst taxying. The
records of 17 SFTS show that on 30 November 1944 trainees at
this School included seventy-four Turkish, five Belgian, four Iraqi,
nine Persian, one Norwegian, one Swedish and two Chinese
nationals in addition to RAF and Commonwealth Air Force trainees.

From December 1944 Vickers Wellingtons started to replace
Ansons, all of which had gone by March 1945. The Wellington
was better suited to training Air Gunners as, unlike the Botha and
Anson which had dorsal turrets it was equipped with a four gun
rear turret similar to those in the heavy bombers then in   operational
use.

Since 10 Air Gunnery School commenced training at Castle
Kennedy in August 1941, training facilities and methods had
advanced. The Boulton Paul Defiant used initially carried only a
pilot and one trainee gunner on each flight. The Blackburn Botha
followed by the Avro Anson were each equipped with a two gun
dorsal gun turret. They carried a gunnery instructor and up to four
trainees on each flight. Gunnery training flights by Bothas, Ansons
and Wellingtons were normally of sixty to ninety minutes duration
and were usually confined to a radius of ten miles from base. These
aircraft carried a pilot, an instructor and, in a Wellington, up to six
trainees. In 1944 each trainee completing a course would in addition

to ground training have at least twenty-five hours' flying time during which he would have fired about five thousand rounds at a drogue target. He would also have had cine-camera gun training and experience in air to ground (or sea) firing.

On 14 June 1945 a gamekeeper leaving his cottage at Lagafater Lodge found a seriously injured airman lying on the pathway leading to the cottage. Though barely conscious, the airman managed to indicate that he had come from an aeroplane which had crashed some distance away. Lagafater Lodge is a shooting lodge in a remote moorland area about seven miles north west of New Luce. The alarm was immediately raised by contacting the civil police who in turn contacted the RAF at Castle Kennedy. A search party and an ambulance were soon on the scene to find that a US Air Force Liberator, which had been reported to be missing over thirty six hours previously, had crashed on Pildinny Hill, 1200 feet above sea level and almost two miles from Lagafater Lodge.

Two further seriously injured survivors were found together with seventeen bodies. The injured men were taken to Lochnaw Hospital and the bodies to Castle Kennedy before being handed over to the US Air Force Base at Prestwick. There is no record of the eventual fate of the three survivors.

It transpired that the Liberator from US Air Force 448th Bomber Group based at Seething, near Norwich was flying to Prestwick when it went missing - it had crashed on Pildinny Hill when flying in low cloud about thirty miles from its destination. A full ground or airborne search had not been mounted as the cloud base had been consistently under one thousand feet for more than forty eight hours.

The men aboard the Liberator were described simply as "American Servicemen". In the immediate post-war period the US Air Force, in common with the RAF, used Liberators for air trooping. The commodious bomb-bay could be readily converted for passenger carrying by fitting lateral canvas seating to accommodate up to twenty men. It is likely that fifteen or more of those aboard this aircraft were passengers in transit to the US Forces base at Prestwick.

When the war in Europe ended in May 1945 training had already slowed down with the reduction in demand for replacement aircrews. Courses in hand were completed allowing 3 AGS to be disbanded on 21 June 1945.

The airfield was immediately taken over by 57 Maintenance Unit, Wig Bay as 104 Sub-Storage Unit to store surplus aircraft. Fifteen Wellingtons were in store at the end of June but the main storage was of De Havilland Mosquitoes of which forty-five were held in February 1946. Most of these were sold as scrap after removal of armament, radar etc. A few Mosquitoes were prepared for delivery to the Turkish Air Force where they were undoubtedly flown by Cranwell trained pilots!

The airfield closed at the end of November 1946 though it did have a further short lease of life a few years later in a civil capacity. On 17 February 1955 the first aircraft to use the airfield for over nine years was a Douglas Dakota of Silver City Airways making a trial run for a proposed service between Castle Kennedy and Newtonards near Belfast.

On 7 April 1955 this Stranraer-Belfast service was inaugurated when a Dakota and a Bristol Freighter 170 made return flights between Castle Kennedy and Newtonards. The Bristol Freighter which carried either three cars and twenty passengers or forty-eight passengers, then maintained a service of three return services six days a week, each crossing having a flight time of twenty minutes. On peak days during July and August up to fourteen crossings were made each day. During the winter months of 1955-56 one daily service operated.

From 6 August 1956 until late September a Bristol Freighter 170 operated a twenty-five minute flight time daily return service between Castle Kennedy and Ronaldsway, Isle of Man. From 1 June 1957 this Manx service operated four trips each week until the end of the holiday season.

Both Belfast and Ronaldsway services appeared to be operating successfully but Silver City Airways, apparently under pressure to extend their English Channel services, ceased all operations from Castle Kennedy at the end of 1957.

CHAPTER 15

RAF STATION, WIGTOWN

An airfield site on farmland at Baldoon one-and-a-half miles south of Wigtown was selected in 1938. The original intention was that this site would be used by target towing aircraft for the Anti-Aircraft Gunnery School being set up at Burrowhead fourteen miles south of Wigtown. However as shown in the chapter on West Freugh the target towing aircraft went to this already-established airfield.

The Baldoon site was not developed until after the outbreak of war; construction work commenced in mid-1940. Perhaps the most significant event during the construction period occurred on the afternoon of 11 July 1941 when workers were permitted to "down tools" for ninety minutes to attend a concert given in a newly built hangar by Gracie Fields who arrived in some style in a Rolls Royce driven by her husband Monty Banks. The local press later described her performance as 'a sheer delight' and her comedy as being 'in the highest degree a masterpiece of clowning'.

No 1 Air Observer School opened on 19 August 1941. The first aircraft, Bristol Blenheims and Blackburn Bothas, arrived on 13 September followed a few days later by Westland Lysanders used to tow targets for air to air gunnery practice. The first training course with forty trainees commenced before the end of September.

One of the main contractors during the construction of the airfield was Airwork Ltd. In order to ease RAF manpower pressures this firm was retained by the Air Ministry as civilian contractors carrying out all aircraft maintenance, catering and general administrative duties, eventually handing over to the RAF on 28 May 1942. Airfield defence was in the hands of an RAF Ground Gunners Defence Flight which on 1 February 1942 became 2834 Squadron RAF Regiment.

Early in 1942 the first Avro Ansons which would eventually replace Bothas arrived; Blenheims were already being phased out. During February a period of severe weather with snow and very low temperatures was followed by a sudden thaw which caused extensive flooding necessitating evacuation of some living quarters. This coincided with an inspection visit from Sir Harold Howitt, a member of the Air Council, who was apparently impressed by the high level of morale despite the difficult conditions. Morale may have been further boosted on 12 March when a concert party headed by Sir Harry Lauder entertained an audience of six hundred. Yet another boost was given early in April when the first WAAF personnel arrived on the Station! April also saw a visit from Air Chief Marshall Sir Edgar Ludlow-Hewitt, Inspector General of the RAF. During March the name of the School was changed to 1 (Observer) Advanced Flying Unit. Training courses for Navigators and Bomb Aimers followed the same lines as those described in the notes on 4 (Observer) Advanced Flying Unit at West Freugh.

In September 1942 airfield facilities were listed as :-

Runways	1200 yards x 50 yards 323° - 143°
	1700 yards x 50 yards 233° - 053°
Petrol Storage	144000 gallons aviation
	6000 gallons motor transport
Oil Storage	7000 gallons
Bomb Storage	264 tons
Small Arms Ammunition	2000000 rounds

Wigtown appears to have been particularly prone to flying accidents, possibly due to the hazards created by nearby high ground; Cairnharrow five miles east from the runways is 1500 feet high; from there contour lines to the north and north-west rarely fall below 1,000 feet and reach over 2,700 feet. In the period between 19 March and 22 August 1942 eight fatal accidents involving Anson, Blenheim and Botha aircraft occurred with thirty lives lost. In one accident on 29 July an Anson crashed into the Solway Firth twelve miles east of Kirkcudbright. An air sea rescue launch from 55 Air Sea Rescue Unit at Kirkcudbright was quickly at the scene of the crash but only the pilot was rescued alive. One of the four lost was an Air Training Corps cadet from the Dumfries ATC Squadron which was spending one week in camp at Wigtown. In a meeting with a Wing Commander Medical Officer from Flying Training Command who visited Wigtown on 29 August 1942 the Senior Medical Officer at Wigtown, a Squadron Leader, expressed his concern about the frequency of aircraft crashes. In the immediately preceding twenty-one days aircraft from Wigtown had been involved in four fatal accidents causing seventeen deaths and ten minor flying accidents without serious casualty. The Squadron Leader noted that a high proportion of the sixty or so pilots flying from the Unit were from Australia, Canada, New Zealand and other colonies, together with a relatively high number of Polish pilots. He believed that these pilots in particular, though he did not exempt British pilots, were unhappy flying on the monotonous and exacting duties required on a training unit. They had come to Britain with the sole intent of flying operationally and their frustration at failing to achieve this objective led to carelessness and risk-taking, for example unauthorised low flying, which led to a higher than necessary risk of accident. He also pointed out that at this time it was the practice to transfer only one pilot each month to operational duties, a practice which did not encourage patient waiting for transfer.

Analysis of the flying records at Wigtown show that between 19 August 1941 and 15 October 1945 twenty-seven aircraft crashed with the loss of sixty-seven lives. Twenty of these crashes were within fifteen minutes' flying time of base and half of them were on the high ground previously referred to. The aircraft involved were twenty-two Ansons, three Lysanders, one Botha and one Blenheim.

The airfield at Wigtown lies within the Parish of Kirkinner; today there remain in Kirkinner Churchyard twenty-three war graves which are the last resting place of one Czechoslovak, eleven Royal Air Force, eight Royal Canadian Air Force and three Royal Australian Air Force airmen.

On 7 July 1942 the Headquarters of 29 Group Training Command, the Group which controlled flying training airfields throughout Scotland moved from Market Drayton to Cargen House, Dumfries. On 9 August 1942 an entry in the Group records reads 'An Infra-Red bombing target is to be sited near New Galloway in near future.' A further entry on 10 October reads 'No 1 (0) AFU

Wigtown made 96 practice IR bombing runs in September. A new IR target will be installed near Wigtown shortly.'

A detailed check of 1 (0) AFU records revealed no record of trainee Bomb Aimers using Infra-Red techniques, nor did the records of 4 (0) AFU West Freugh. It has now been ascertained with the help of the RAF Museum, Hendon that infra-red bombing was used only as a training aid. Infra-red lights shining vertically upward were placed on target sites. Aircraft on simulated bombing runs carried cameras loaded with film sensitive to infra-red light with a mechanism which opened the shutter when the simulated bomb was due to hit the target. When developed the film enabled an assessment of bombing accuracy to be made. It has not been possible to trace the location of the infra-red targets at New Galloway and at Wigtown nor of a later one said to be situated near Whithorn. As Group records do not comment on IR bombing training in use elsewhere it seems that 1 (0) AFU was the only Unit within the group using this system.

1 (0) AFU used a number of conventional targets on which 11lb smoke bombs were dropped allowing the smoke plume to be plotted by two nearby sighting posts from which quadrant bearings were taken to assess the bomb aimers' proficiency. One of these targets was located offshore on the west side of Wigtown Bay between Cruggleton and Portyerrock with sighting posts situated on the cliff top. Another land based target was located north of Elrig Village with three others within a few miles of Kirkcowan at Drumwalt, Dirnow and Shennanton.

Two other targets were used occasionally by 1 (0) AFU but primarily by 10 (0) AFU Dumfries were located just off shore in the Solway Firth at Carsethorn and Sandyhills.

Many, but not all of the ranges had at a distance of about one mile a large white painted arrow pointing directly at the target as an aid to bomb aimers in the early part of their training.

On 4 November 1942 an Anson on a night navigation training exercise over Northern Ireland encountered thick fog on the return leg of the flight. A coincidental electrical failure meant that the aircraft wireless and all lights lost power with the result that they were unable to find Wigtown. Turning back towards Northern

27. RAF Station Wigtown, 8th October, 1942, from 2000 feet.   *RAFM W1/12/5*

28. RAF war graves, Kirkinner Cemetery   Author

Ireland hoping to find clear weather they spotted the lights of a ship with which the Wireless Operator managed to make contact using a signal torch. As they were now running short of fuel the pilot ditched the Anson as close to the ship as prevailing conditions permitted. Within twenty minutes they were picked up by the vessel - a trawler heading for Fleetwood where they were landed next morning.

During November 1942 flying hours at 1 (O) AFU were one thousand two hundred and thirty-six day and one thousand one hundred and eighty-one night, a total of two thousand four hundred and seventeen hours with an aircraft complement of fifty-six Ansons, thirteen Bothas and seven Lysanders. A letter of commendation was received from Flying Training Command as November was the first month in which over one thousand hours' night flying had been achieved by any one Unit in the Command. It should be added that a similar commendation was also received by units at Jurby on the Isle of Man, Millom in Cumberland and West Freugh who had all exceeded one thousand hours in November; the West Freugh figure was one thousand and forty-seven hours. As these units are all around the Solway Firth area the inference must be that night weather conditions were good in November!

Training of Navigators and Bomb Aimers continued, trainees including number of Canadians and Australians. In August 1943 flying hours for the month were three thousand seven hundred and forty-two with a complement of sixty-five Ansons and nine Lysanders.

In the summer and autumn months of 1943 Hawker Hurricanes, Supermarine Spitfires and Hawker Typhoons of 2nd Tactical Air Force were regularly carrying out aggressive daylight sweeps over Northern France attacking any military target which presented itself. Typhoons equipped with four 20 mm cannons acquired a reputation as "train busters". Three Typhoon Squadrons actively involved were 174 based at Lydd, Kent, 175 based at Westhampnett, Chichester and 182 based at New Romney, Kent. On 17 September 1943 eight aircraft from each of these squadrons were detailed to take part in Operation Nimbus, an invasion training exercise taking place in southern Scotland. On 18 September the twenty-four Typhoons under command of the Group Captain Station Commander at Lydd flew from their bases, refuelling en route at Hawarden, North Wales, arriving at Wigtown during the afternoon accompanied by three Lockheed Hudsons and one Handley Page Harrow as support aircraft.

The Hawker Typhoon 1b with a 2200 hp Napier Sabre engine had a maximum speed of 412 mph when armed with four 20mm cannon and two 500lb bombs.

Learning that they would not be taking part in Nimbus until 21 September the Operation Record Books of all three Squadrons describe 19 and 20 September as days of relaxation concentrating on "boozing in the Officers' Mess". 175 Squadron reported that on 20 September the Wigtown Station Intelligence Officer set out in a Jeep to visit Garlieston, Isle of Whithorn and Port William, returning with thirty-four lobsters which created an ample lobster and beer repast in the Mess that night.

On the morning of 21 September six Typhoons from 182 Squadron flew to Turnberry, Ayrshire to be briefed for Operation Nimbus. They were told that they were to cover the withdrawal of troops from beaches at Ardlamont, Kyles of Bute, by dropping smoke bombs. Fifteen Typhoons from 174 and 175 Squadrons left Wigtown in early afternoon flying north to join the six from 182 Squadron. These twenty-one aircraft each dropped two 500 lb smoke bombs on the beaches over a period of forty-five minutes creating a tremendous volume of smoke. The OC Troops, who had monitored the exercise from a Royal Navy Frigate lying just off-shore, later congratulated them on the accuracy of their bombing which had fully obscured the withdrawal.

That night prior to departure from Wigtown on the following morning a farewell party was held in the Officers' Mess. This was described as being a complete shambles! The pilots all left foot imprints in soot cemented with beer on the Mess ceiling; all of them, including the Group Captain, were said to be covered in soot from head to foot.

The Typhoons engaged in Operation Nimbus were dependent on 3206 Servicing Commando for servicing whilst at Wigtown. This recent concept consisted of a full team of all the various ground staff tradesmen required to keep an operational Squadron flying who, in addition to their trade skills, had completed full Commando training. The intention was that Units of this nature would work literally with a spanner in one hand and a Sten gun in the other, supporting aircraft operating close to enemy lines, a situation envisaged likely in the aftermath of an invasion of Europe. They wore khaki battledress displaying their RAF insignia alongside the Commando badge.

In his book 'The Guinea Pigs' published in 1983 Raymond Foxall describes Commando Training thus:-

'A member of a commando unit was trained in unarmed combat and to be a crack shot with all types of small arms. He had to be capable of marching thirty miles a day over rough country in full equipment. Every man was required to be able to swim a specified distance in full kit and with his rifle kept above water. So rigourous was the training that only five per cent of the men volunteering for commando units reached the physical standard and military efficiency demanded.'

3206 Commando records show their base only as 121 Airfield later ascertained to be Westhampnett, the base of 175 Squadron. The journey to Wigtown was considered to be an excellent training opportunity. Leaving Westhampnett on 16 September they travelled north in Bedford trucks, later said to be in very poor condition. The first night was spent at Catterick, continuing next day to Dumfries before arriving at Wigtown at midday on 18 September. On arrival they did not pitch tents as anticipated as they were given the use of four Blister hangars as accommodation, cookhouse etc. A hot meal was supplied on arrival, thereafter they were given rations to prepare their own meals. The Unit Log is noted "Food seems to be in short supply here". A stark contrast with the beer and lobster diet in the Officers' Mess!

On 19 and 20 September routine inspection and maintenance was carried out on the twenty-four Typhoons; then, on 21 September, the twenty-one planes involved in Nimbus were each loaded with two 500 lb smoke bombs. Next day all necessary servicing was completed before all twenty-four Typhoons left during the morning to return to their bases.

The return journey starting on 23 September took four days with overnight stops at Carlisle, Doncaster and Stevenage before arriving at Westhampnett on 26 September. For the record, 3206 Servicing Commando embarked on a tank landing craft at Gosport on 13 June 1944, one week after the D-Day landings in Normandy They landed 'in Normandy' at 1100 hours on 14 June and moved immediately to 'an airfield in France' where they were joined on 17 June by 'aircraft from 121 Airfield'. As noted earlier 121 Airfield was the base of 175 Squadron at Westhampnett in Sussex.

As previously mentioned the high ground to the north and east of Wigtown led to aircraft crashes with 1 (O) AFU being called upon to provide search and rescue parties. In addition to searches for aircraft flying from Wigtown, searches for other missing aircraft were carried out on sixteen occasions in the three years between September 1942 and September 1945. The aircraft involved included four Ansons, one Royal Navy Hellcat, one Liberator, one Mustang, one Thunderbolt and one Typhoon. Thirty-eight bodies were recovered.

This involved a considerable strain on manpower resources. In mountainous country with few roads, searches could take several days and could involve up to one hundred men. Eventually in early 1944 a specialised Mountain Rescue Unit was set up with thirty volunteer members who were trained by a Sergeant from an Army Mountain Division who was attached to RAF Wigtown for several weeks. An Austrian and former member of the Alpine Corps, he was an expert mountaineer who was able to impart his expertise in mountain navigation, methods of search and casualty evacuation. Specialised equipment including four-wheel drive vehicles, sledge stretchers and "walkie talkie" wireless communication equipment was now made available.

On 2 May 1944 a party of journalists was invited to see a demonstration by the Unit. After censorship clearance a number of national papers published reports. The 'Daily Express' praised the work of "a Unit based at an RAF Station in south west Scotland operating in mountainous country within a forty-mile radius of base".

Wigtown, in common with most other RAF airfields had a resident Padre. In June 1944 a new Padre named Arthur H Procter arrived. Arthur Procter, who was born in Bootle, Lancashire in 1890, served as a private in The King's (Liverpool) Regiment in World War I. On 4 June 1916, though under heavy enemy fire, he rescued two wounded men who were lying in full view of the German trenches some 75 yards in front of the British trenches. He dressed their wounds and managed to get them under cover from where they were rescued when darkness had fallen. For this action, he was awarded the Victoria Cross. Leaving the Army in 1919 he was ordained in 1927 later serving as an RAF chaplain throughout World War II. He died in Sheffield in January 1973.

Between 6.30 and 7.15 am on 27 August 1944 many of the good burghers of Wigtown were awakened by unaccustomed aircraft noise over Baldoon. Those who looked out into the morning light saw ten Avro Lancasters circuiting and landing. The story commences on the previous day when thirteen Lancasters of 463 Squadron Royal Australian Air Force based at Waddington, Lincolnshire were detailed to bomb Königsberg, the capital city of East Prussia.

The city was being used by the German forces as a distribution centre for supplies for the Russian front sixty miles to the east. Konigsberg, which is now called Kaliningrad, stands at the mouth of the River Pregel on the east side of the Gulf of Danzig. This was the first time that Bomber Command had visited this area and it was one of the longest trips which the Command had undertaken. All thirteen aircraft carried maximum fuel load and each had the same bomb load - one 2000 lb high explosive bomb and twelve 500 lb incendiary clusters. Take off from Waddington was between 8.10 and 8.40 pm; by 11pm three aircraft had returned to base with mechanical or electrical faults. The remaining ten bombed the target under the control of a "master bomber" of 83 (Pathfinder) Squadron flying from Coningsby, Lincolnshire who was already over the target. On the return journey fires at the target remained visible for two hundred miles.

By now weather conditions had closed virtually every airfield in eastern England so, when over the North Sea, 463 Squadron was advised by wireless to divert to Wigtown where all ten planes landed safely - having been airborne for around eleven hours and having flown some 1,800 miles they had fuel for only thirty to forty minutes' duration left. Regrettably they were not accompanied by the Pathfinder Lancaster of 83 Squadron which had been shot down by a Messerschmitt Me110, crashing near Vejle in Denmark. Only the pilot and the bomb aimer surviving to spend the remainder of the war in a Stalag Luft prison camp. As soon as conditions at Waddington permitted, the Station Commander flew to Wigtown in one of two Lancasters which carried twenty-two personnel - most of them Intelligence Officers to de-brief the crews. By 7 pm on 27 August all twelve Lancasters had returned to Waddington from where the Station Commander signalled his thanks to his opposite number at Wigtown.

Throughout 1944 and into 1945 training of Navigators and Bomb Aimers by 1 (O) AFU continued apace, carrying on until the final course ended in October 1945 allowing the Unit to be disbanded on 12 November 1945.

Two weeks later on 1 December the airfield buildings were taken over by 220 Maintenance Unit, Dumfries as 30 Sub Storage Site. This Maintenance Unit which handled clothing and barrack (ie domestic) stores had, during the war years, acquired from its Dumfries Headquarters storage sites as far afield as Selkirk and Glasgow. Now as requisitioned premises were returned to their former owners, stocks held were transferred to Wigtown pending disposal. 14 Maintenance Unit, Carlisle took over 30 Sub Storage Site on 20 June 1946 when 220 Maintenance Unit closed down. Over the following eighteen months Wigtown stocks were gradually moved by rail to other Maintenance Units. Throughout this period staffing was mainly civilian with a Flight Lieutenant in charge of a small RAF contingent. Seventy-five civilian staff in July 1946 had fallen to five in January 1948 when the Sub Storage Unit finally closed down.

In June 1947 the Bombing Trials Unit took up temporary residence at Wigtown where it remained until returning to West Freugh in May 1948. Whilst at Wigtown flying three Avro Lancasters, two De Havilland Mosquitoes and one Hawker Tempest, BTU continued with bombing, rocket, airborne radar and other trials using the Luce Bay and Braid Fell ranges. It also accepted responsibility for the Wigtown based Mountain Rescue Unit.

With the departure of the Bombing Trials Unit the few RAF personnel remaining at Wigtown were quickly dispersed, leaving the Station to close down on 15 July 1948.

CHAPTER 16

RAF STATION, KIDSDALE

Notes on West Freugh record how in the summer of 1938 and again from May 1939 target towing aircraft of E Flight, 1 Anti-Aircraft Co-operation Unit were based at West Freugh to provide target towing facilities for 2 Heavy Anti Aircraft Practice Camp at Burrowhead near Isle of Whithorn.

On 8 May 1939 W Flight of this Unit left Biggin Hill in Kent in a ten vehicle convoy which arrived at Burrowhead on 10 May. The following day two De Havilland Tiger Moths together with a Miles Magister landed on a grass strip which had been prepared at Kidsdale two miles to the north west of Burrowhead.

The Magister, which was to be the Flight communications plane, was flown by the Flight Commanding Officer. The two Tiger Moths were not in fact what they first appeared but were Queen Bees - Tiger Moths adapted to fly under radio control as targets for trainee gunners firing 3.7 inch anti-aircraft guns.

The Flight with some fifty personnel commanded by a Squadron Leader was housed under canvas alongside the Royal Artillery camp pending completion of permanent buildings which were under construction at Kidsdale. The original intention was that the airmen would remain under canvas at Burrowhead travelling to Kidsdale as necessary - a six mile road journey - until the end of the Royal Artillery Territorial camp season in September. The permanent buildings at Kidsdale were planned to be ready for occupation in May 1940 when W Flight would return with the commencement of another summer camp season for the Territorial Army trainee gunners. The outbreak of war in September 1939 necessarily changed these plans. 2 Heavy Anti-Aircraft Practice Camp now became a permanent unit and W Flight were required to remain where they were.

From the outbreak of war the airfield at Kidsdale was guarded by soldiers from Burrowhead until October 1940, when this duty was taken over by RAF Ground Gunners of 276 (Defence) Flight which on 1 February 1942 became 2766 Squadron, RAF Regiment.

With the advent of winter weather, living conditions in the two-man bell tents with messes, stores and other facilities in marquees, became to say the least, uncomfortable. For some weeks a church hall in Whithorn, five miles from Burrowhead, was used as sleeping accommodation until on 1 December all personnel moved into the as yet incomplete buildings at Kidsdale. Rough and ready conditions were considerably worsened when in January and February 1940 severe snow storms hit south west Scotland. Road and rail communications were completely severed, food stocks were virtually exhausted before Burrowhead was re-supplied by an air drop.

Meantime, weather permitting, Queen Bee flights over the guns continued after the first "shoot" which was on 7 June 1939. Before the first pilotless flight and at regular intervals thereafter, each Queen Bee was test flown by one of the two pilots on the staff of W Flight. During this test the aircraft was flown manually using the dual control system which was fitted in addition to the radio controlled auto-pilot then subjected to a lengthy series of tests to check response to radio signals sent by the ground controller. These responses were monitored by the pilot up to a range of thirty miles from ground control. Only when the responses were wholly accurate was the aircraft cleared for pilotless operation.

Radio control equipment weighing 1,500 lb was housed in a three-ton truck. The Flight Controller, usually W Flight Commanding Officer, operated from a position in the gun park on the cliff top from which he had a clear view of the area in which the Queen Bee would fly. He was connected by land line to an operator in the radio control truck who in turn was connected by land line to the transmitter, which had two seventy foot masts, at Kidsdale.

Signals to the aircraft were in Morse code - a series of dots and dashes which were normally wholly accurate but could be subject to radio interference requiring the controller to be vigilant lest the aircraft performed an unexpected manoeuvre caused by a false signal. Signals received passed to an autopilot which operated compressed air valves linked to elevators, rudder and throttle. The Queen Bee was always kept within visibility limits and normally flew at a height of not more than 12,000 feet.

From the first flight in June 1939 until March 1940 all radio controlled flights were made from Burrowhead. The Queen Bees were fitted with floats for sea landing. They were launched from a catapult, of the type used by the Royal Navy for ship board launches using steam power, which was now adapted to be fired by a cordite charge. On completion of a flight the Queen Bee was landed in the sea where it was met and made secure by an RAF launch based in Isle of Whithorn harbour. A small steam coaster, the *Crescent*, which had been leased by the RAF, picked up the Queen Bee, hoisted it inboard, then proceeded to the Isle of Whithorn where the Queen Bee was hoisted on to the pier.

A waiting team of fitters and riggers now removed the wings and floats which were stowed on a three ton truck. The floats were replaced by a standard Tiger Moth undercarriage, the tail skid was secured to the rear of the truck and the Queen Bee towed on its own wheels along the public roads to Burrowhead just over two miles distant. Here the whole process was reversed, wings were refitted, undercarriage removed and floats reinstated before the Queen Bee could be lifted on to the catapult prior to the next launch. This was clearly a cumbersome and time consuming exercise; thus no-one was sorry when in March 1940 it was learned that a system for take off and landing from grass runways had been developed and approved, allowing all future radio controlled flights to be from the grass strip at Kidsdale.

Take off from grass involved tethering the Queen Bee to a secure point whilst the engine was run up, then severing the tether at the appropriate moment for a radio controlled take off. Landing technique was similar to that used at sea; the aircraft was brought towards the landing strip in a controlled glide until a twenty-five foot trailing aerial struck the ground triggering a device which cut the engine with the aircraft at a height of about ten feet.

W Flight necessarily worked in close co-operation with E Flight at West Freugh whose target towing aircraft were over the

29. De Havilland Queen Bee on launching catapult at Burrowhead, July 1938.   *RAFM P1580*

30. De Havilland Queen Bee undertow by RAF launch, Isle of Whithorn   *Mrs. C. M. Millar*

guns daily, given suitable weather conditions. Drogues towed by Hawker Henleys and Boulton Paul Defiants both with Rolls Royce Merlin engines of over 1,000 hp passed over the guns at speeds of around 200 mph which could not be equalled by the Queen Bees with a 130 hp De Havilland Gypsy Major engine giving a speed of little more than 100 mph. The Queen Bees could however take evasive action which the drogues could not emulate. Records show that between 15 August 1939 and 13 February 1942 eleven Queen Bees were shot down by the Royal Artillery Gunners and another thirteen were lost in crashes at least seven of which were attributed to gun-fire damage. On average the life of a Queen Bee was eight 'shoots' before loss or write off.

The one-hundredth Queen Bee shoot was reached on 21 May 1941 giving an average of one shoot each week since 7 June 1939. Night flights were made occasionally; take off was made about two hours before dawn which allowed reasonable visibility for landing. On 9 July 1941 W Flight claimed a record when a Queen Bee was flown at a height of 14,000 feet which exceeded De Havilland's stated maximum operational height by 600 feet.

On Sunday 23 November 1941, morning service at Sorbie Parish Church, Millisle was drawing to a close when the congregation heard a loud explosion nearby. Emerging from the church they learned that a large aircraft had exploded in mid-air before crashing in Garlieston Bay about one mile off-shore. The crash was seen by Creetown Observer Corps Post whose report instigated an immediate search for survivors. W Flight Magister which was called out to search, quickly located floating debris. The Flight launch from Isle of Whithorn was guided to the scene where they recovered the bodies of the two crew, members of Air Transport Auxiliary, who had been flying a Consolidated Liberator on a delivery flight from the transatlantic terminal at Prestwick. The bodies were landed at Garlieston where an ambulance from RAF Station Wigtown was waiting. The Flight Engineer, a United States citizen, was buried at Kirkinner on 26 November.

Queen Bee flights continued into 1942 though no longer considered to be viable; the last flight was in early May before W Flight was disbanded on 10 May 1942. For the next three months the strip at Kidsdale was unused. 651 Air Observation Post Squadron which had been based at Old Sarum, Wiltshire, for some time was detached to RAF Station Dumfries in July 1942. At the end of July the Squadron became involved in a large Army excercise which was based around Ecclefechan some twelve miles east of Dumfries. Squadron Headquarters were set up in Ecclefechan and their Taylorcraft planes flew from a number of Royal Artillery bases including an RAF range at Langholm. When this excercise ended ten days later the Squadron were instructed to move to Kidsdale where they arrived on 11 August with seven Taylorcraft. The Squadron took over Glasserton House three miles from Kidsdale as their Headquarters where they remained for eight weeks before moving into accommodation at Kidsdale. As with other Air Observation Post Squadrons all pilots were experienced Royal Artillery officers who had completed full RAF training as pilots. The Commanding Officer of 651 Squadron was a Royal Artillery Major, the Adjutant an RAF Flight Lieutenant; all ground crew were RAF personnel. Within days of arrival, on 22 August, mobilisation orders for service overseas were received. Preparation for embarkation occupied the next few weeks, for example several flights were made to the Taylorcraft factory at Leicester to pick up spares.

During October planes from the Squadron took part in exercises Honeymoon, Eskimo and Igloo of which little is recorded except that they involved spotting for Artillery units exercising in north east England.

During November the Squadron aircraft now comprising twelve Taylorcraft were apparently stripped down, crated, then moved by road to Liverpool for embarkation. The final Kidsdale entry in the Squadron Log is dated 23 November; the next entry dated 1 April 1943 is in Egypt. On 26 November all accommodation at Kidsdale was handed over to the Royal Artillery at Burrowhead for their use. Glasserton House was subsequently used by Royal Engineers from the Mulberry Harbour site at Cairnhead near Isle of Whithorn.

CHAPTER 17

14 EMBARKATION UNIT, STRANRAER

Since 1849 when the Post Office commenced using the Stranraer to Larne route for the Irish mail a regular cross channel service has been maintained. Following the outbreak of war this route acquired greater importance as large numbers of servicemen were based in Northern Ireland. Movement control for troops and for military freight was established in August 1939; then as volumes increased 14 Embarkation Unit was formed at Stranraer on 9 August 1940 to handle RAF movements.

By 1 September a Movement Control Office had been established at the harbour with a staff of seven. One of the first freight movements they had to tackle was the shipping of supplies of hydrogen required for two RAF Balloon Squadrons which were about to move to Northern Ireland. On 8 September forty hydrogen trailers designed to carry high pressure gas cylinders were "detrained and shipped", a task taking five-and-a-half hours to complete.

On 15 September 968 Balloon Squadron, which had arrived in Belfast on 12 September, had fourteen balloons flying. On 25 September twenty personnel with four vehicles from 920 Balloon Squadron crossed from Stranraer to Larne en route from Kyle of Lochalsh to Londonderry. The bulk of their equipment including balloons was shipped direct from Glasgow to Londonderry where a few days later they had sixteen balloons flying. Both Squadrons were commanded by Wing Commanders; normal balloon complement was between thirty and forty per Squadron.

Regular shipments of hydrogen cylinders continued thereafter, travelling from Billingham in County Durham by rail to Stranraer, thence by sea to Larne. Hydrogen manufacturing capacity in Britain at this time could barely meet the demands of industry plus the requirements of the many balloon barrages then in existence.

31. Balloon barrage. 920 Balloon Squadron, RAF

The Air Ministry therefore authorised all RAF Balloon Squadrons to use locally produced coal gas up to a maximum of forty per cent of capacity when inflating balloons. As hydrogen is fourteen times lighter than air, some adulteration was acceptable, particularly as coal gas then produced contained a fairly high proportion of hydrogen in addition to methane and carbon monoxide. The only Balloon Squadron which did not use this adulteration process were those in and around London where coal gas was in comparatively short supply due to air raid damage to gas works and to distribution mains.

However there were problems in Northern Ireland which has no natural supply of coal. Gas supplies had always been produced by shipping in coal from the coalfields in Ayrshire and Cumberland. As importing capacity was severely limited by wartime conditions no supply of gas was available for the Balloon Squadrons. Neither was any surplus capacity available from a number of small gasworks within around 40 miles of Stranraer. Eventually a supply was found to be available from Kilmarnock which is 65 road miles from Stranraer. Extra drivers were attached to the Embarkation Unit to drive Dodge trucks with trailers to transport cylinders of coal gas on two return journeys each week between Stranraer and Kilmarnock. The road between Stranraer and Girvan was not in the winter of 1940-41 ideal for heavy vehicles particularly along the cliff top at Bennane Head near Ballantrae. One driver was killed here when his truck loaded with empty cylinders skidded over the edge.

By early November the Unit had a Squadron Leader in charge with seventeen other staff. At the end of December 1940 the ships on the Station were *Princess Maud* and *Princess Margaret*, the two pre-war Stranraer vessels which now carried all civilian passengers and freight with some service traffic, together with *Duchess of Hamilton, Royal Daffodil, Maid of Orleans, Biarritz* and *Canterbury*, all passenger vessels; *Twickenham Ferry, Shepperton Ferry* and *Hampton Ferry* carried freight. These last eight vessels carried only service traffic; most of them had before the war been on cross channel routes to France. The three "*Ferry*" vessels were "drive on" stern loaders able to use the loading ramp installed at Stranraer just before the war.

An indication of the difficulties of travel in wartime conditions is given in the records of 240 Squadron. The Squadron flying boats flew from Loch Ryan to Lough Erne in Northern Ireland on 27 March 1941. The Squadron vehicles and ground crews embarked on the Hampton Ferry between 8 pm and 9 pm on the 27th, sailing for Larne at 4.30 am next day. From Larne they travelled by road to Killadeas on Lough Erne, arriving there at 8 pm - twenty-four hours after embarkation.

On 9 February 1941 the *Princess Maud* reported a machine gun attack by an enemy aircraft when she was in mid channel at 11 pm; no hits were recorded. With hindsight it seems likely that this single burst of fire came from one of the many RAF aircraft then on training flights in this area - the crew being aware that they were over the sea but unaware of the proximity of a nearby, unlighted ship.

On 20 April 1941 the first of many Stirling aircraft fuselages each eighty-seven feet long arrived on a Queen Mary low loader road vehicle from Short Brothers' factory at Rochester, Kent. This was shipped aboard the Hampton Ferry en route to Maghaberry airfield near Lisburn where Short Brothers had a Stirling assembly plant as an out-station of their Sydenham, Belfast factory. By the end of April sixteen similar fuselages had been shipped; thereafter regular shipments continued for over twelve months. Being shipped in the opposite direction at this time were Churchill tanks built by Harland & Wolf in Belfast which were passed on by rail from Stranraer to have their armament fitted.

In July 1941 RAF personnel movements were six thousand two hundred and thirty-eight outwards and four thousand one hundred and one inwards; vehicle movements were three hundred and fifty-four outwards and three hundred and thirty inwards. In the year ended 31 July total RAF personnel movements were forty-nine thousand one hundred and ninety-three outwards and thirty-four thousand five hundred and fifty-six inwards. No exact figures are available but it is understood the RAF movements were about forty per cent of all military traffic.

The port of Stranraer came to a standstill in January 1942 when from 21st to 23rd heavy snow falls stopped all movements by rail and by sea. During May 1942 a number of US Air Force personnel were landed at Stranraer; on 17 May a number who had arrived in Belfast Lough aboard *SS Cuba* were disembarked by tender and brought direct to Stranraer followed on 25 May by a number disembarked by tender from *MV Arundel Castle* lying at anchor at the mouth of Loch Ryan. On 16 July 1942 *Shepperton Ferry* was discharged using a temporary ramp to test facilities at 2 Military Port then still under construction at Cairnryan.

The first WAAF personnel were clerks who joined the Unit in March 1943. They were accommodated in Craignelder, a large house adjacent to the harbour which from 14 August 1943 also housed the Unit Headquarters. Another vessel, *Empress Queen*, joined the Station in January 1944; shortly afterwards in February and March respectively *Twickenham Ferry* and *Hampton Ferry* were withdrawn for service elsewhere. Freight traffic having considerably reduced in volume, *Shepperton Ferry* was also withdrawn on 16 June 1944.

As the war drew to a close, troop movements also decreased in number. *Duchess of Hamilton* was withdrawn in August 1945; she was temporarily replaced by *St Seriol* until 28 November when she too was withdrawn. In October 1945 RAF personnel movements outward and inward totalled 15,942, many of whom were inward bound heading for demobilisation. Over the following few months the workload of the Unit reduced quickly allowing it to be closed down on 28 February 1946. Thereafter for as long as remained necessary RAF personnel and freight movements were handled by the Army Embarkation Unit which still operated at Stranraer Harbour. The *Empress Queen* remained at Stranraer as a troop ship until 6 October 1946, assisted during February and March 1946 by the *Duchess of Hamilton.*

CHAPTER 18

55 AIR SEA RESCUE UNIT, KIRKCUDBRIGHT

As flying training facilities around the Solway Firth expanded, additional Air Sea Rescue services were required in this area. Part of this requirement was met when 55 Air Sea Rescue Marine Craft Unit was opened on 23 March 1942 at Gibb Hill on the Dee Estuary two miles south of Kirkcudbright. The Unit, equipped with two pinnaces, was commanded by a Flight Lieutenant. The parent station which provided back-up services such as accounting (pay!) and medical services, was RAF Station, Silloth, Cumberland until August when this was changed to the nearer RAF Station Wigtown.

A twenty-four hour watch was maintained with one boat always at immediate readiness. To avoid any risk of being stranded at low water the duty boat was moored in sheltered deep water off Ross Island at the mouth of the estuary.

The first crash call was answered on 21 June when one body was recovered from a plane which had crashed off Southerness Point seven miles east of Ross Island. Over the next thirty-two months, thirty-four crash calls were answered; twelve aircrew members were rescued but unfortunately on only two calls were crews rescued without loss; on most calls the report read "no survivors". In February 1943 a third pinnace was brought in to ensure adequate cover for the area of operation - the whole of the Solway Firth east of a line from Burrowhead, Wigtownshire to St Bees Head, Cumberland. Some calls were not quite routine; on 16 November 1942 a Consolidated Catalina flying boat which had made a forced landing three miles off Southerness Point was taken in tow to arrive back at base in Loch Ryan after a twelve hour tow. On 18 May 1943 a call was received from Tongland four miles inland from Gibb Hill where a Royal Navy Fairey Swordfish had made a forced landing without injury to the three man crew. A more serious incident occurred on the night of 18 July 1943 when a crash crew travelled by road to Dundrennan village five miles south east of Kirkcudbright where a Bristol Beaufighter had crashed demolishing a house, killing the crew of two together with four civilians.

The final call attended was to a "no survivors" crash off Burrowhead on 19 November 1944.

55 Air Sea Rescue Unit was closed down on 11 December 1944. The buildings remained in the care of RAF Station Wigtown until November 1945 when they were taken over by 220 Maintenance Unit, Dumfries to be used as 29 Sub Storage Site. Twelve hundred square feet of storage space was used to store surplus clothing pending disposal until the site was closed down in June 1946.

CHAPTER 19

SUB STORAGE SITES, TONGLAND
AND KIRKCUDBRIGHT

In March 1939 the Air Ministry decided that 1 Maintenance Unit, which handled the bulk of RAF Barrack Stores, ie clothing and domestic equipment, should be moved to a less vulnerable site than that which it occupied at Kidbrooke in south east London. The Arrol Johnson Motor Company factory in Dumfries was taken over on 20 March 1939 to form "H" Maintenance Unit which incorporated a large part of 1 Maintenance Unit. Renamed 220 Maintenance Unit considerable expansion took place during the war years with over twenty Sub Storage Units being opened in premises as varied as distillery warehouses and woollen mills as far afield as Glasgow and Selkirk with Unit HQ remaining in Dumfries.

One of the Sub Storage Sites was the former Arrol Johnson factory in Tongland near Kirkcudbright and another was in unnamed garage premises in Kirkcudbright. When the European war ended in May 1945 requisitioned premises were returned to their owners as soon as feasible with stores transferred to space becoming surplus in other RAF premises. As recorded in the notes on these Units, 29 Sub Storage Unit was established at the former Air Sea Rescue Unit at Gibb Hill, Kirkcudbright and 30 Sub Storage Unit at RAF Station, Wigtown.

220 Maintenance Unit, Dumfries closed down on 20 June 1946 when the remainder of largely depleted stocks was transferred to 14 Maintenance Unit, Carlisle. The sites at Tongland and Kirkcudbright were returned to their owners at this time.

CHAPTER 20

275 MAINTENANCE UNIT, CAIRNRYAN

Only one RAF Unit was formed in Galloway in post-war years. This was 275 Maintenance Unit formed at 2 Military Port, Cairnryan on 27 November 1945. The purpose of this Unit was defined as "supervision of disposal by deep water dumping of obsolete high explosive and incendiary bombs from RAF Units in Great Britain". The Unit with one hundred and sixty personnel commanded by a Squadron Leader was housed in former Army quarters at Leffnol near Cairnryan.

Dumping commenced in November 1945 using four Tank Landing Craft which were lined with wood to avoid the possibility of sparks causing an explosion. The load of each vessel, determined by bulk as well as weight, was one hundred and sixty tons of small arms ammunition, one hundred and fifty tons of high explosive bombs or one hundred tons of incendiary bombs. All material for dumping arrived at the port by rail on special trains. By March 1946 the Unit strength had increased to three hundred and eighty and a 350-ton Coaster *Sir Evelyn Wood* was in use to dump 500 lb high explosive bombs. In July 1946 up to twelve Tank Landing Craft were in use, some being loaned by a Royal Army Ordnance Corps Unit based at the Military Port, which was also engaged in explosives disposal. The weight dumped in July was fifteen thousand two hundred and eighty-seven tons. In September 1946 SS *Empire Woodlark* was loaded with fourteen hundred tons of "chemical weapons" before being towed out to be scuttled. The Unit strength reached a peak of four hundred and seventy in December 1946; in April 1947 when rehoused at West Freugh the strength had fallen to three hundred and twenty. Dumping operations now slowed down with the final dump of two hundred and thirty-three tons being made on 3 April 1948. During the period 17 November 1945 to 3 April

32. Tank landing craft used for HE bomb disposal, No 2 Military Port, Cairn Ryan

IWM H42201

1948 over one hundred and twenty thousand tons of obsolete explosives were dumped.

275 MU considered that they had been fortunate to carry out their onerous duties without serious mishap. The Royal Army Ordnance Corps team working alongside them at Cairnryan who undoubtedly handled greater quantities of explosive were not so fortunate. On 25 June 1946 an explosion was caused by a box of fuses being dropped into a partially loaded Tank Landing Craft 769. Eight soldiers were killed. Earlier on 8 January 1946 three LCT's loaded with 'ammunition' left Silloth for Cairnryan. The vessels became separated off Burrowhead in deteriorating weather conditions, two of them running for shelter at Ramsey, Isle of Man. The third, LCT 527, with a crew of twelve apparently foundered and was not seen again, though seven bodies of the crew members were recovered from the coastline around Wigtown Bay.

With the task for which it was formed completed, 275 Maintenance Unit was disbanded on 3 May 1948.

One year later in mid 1949, 249 Maintenance Unit, Great Orton, Carlisle sent a detachment of forty men to West Freugh to carry out further dumping operations from 2 Military Port, Cairnryan. Obsolete explosives were received at Cairnryan by road and rail before dumping from Tank Landing Craft. Quantities dumped varied from two hundred and fifty tons to one thousand eight hundred and forty tons per month; the total dumped in 1950 was twenty-one thousand four hundred and ninety tons.

Roles were reversed when on 9 December 1950 a United States Navy vessel, the *Anes Victory*, berthed at Cairnryan to discharge explosives for the United States Air Forces based in Great Britain. From 11 to 14 December the discharge of 2000 lb and 4000 lb bombs on to rail wagons was supervised by 249 MU. This operation was not without consequence as apparently some of the railway wagons used proved to be unserviceable. On 12 December a party of airmen was sent to Creetown railway station to transfer 4000 lb bombs to serviceable wagons and on 14 and 15 December a party transferred 2000 lb bombs at Newton Stewart station.

Dumping continued throughout 1951 with an average of six hundred and thirty-five tons dumped each month giving a total for the year of seven thousand six hundred and twenty-four tons. In 1952 dumping continued until July when 249 Maintenance Unit closed down. The tonnage dumped during the three year period of operation at Cairnryan was thirty-three thousand seven hundred and fifty-four. On 31 July 1952 the seven personnel remaining at West Freugh were transferred to 28 Maintenance Unit, Harpur Hill, Buxton.

Over a period of seven years approximately one hundred and fifty-four thousand tons of explosives were disposed of by RAF units operating from 2 Military Port, Cairnryan. The dumping site for this material was Beaufort's Dyke which is described as 'an elongated depression some 32 nautical miles long north to south and 6½ nautical miles wide east to west with a depth in excess of 120 fathoms at the deepest point seven miles off the Mull of Galloway.' The Dyke is approximately mid-channel and has a depth which varies from one hundred to one hundred and fifty fathoms.

CHAPTER 21

FROM DH6 TO TORNADO

When formed on 1 April 1918 the Royal Air Force had a foothold in Galloway at East Freugh airship station, a foothold retained in 1999 by West Freugh airfield which years ago absorbed East Freugh within it boundaries.

Though the location remains, all else has changed beyond recognition. The seventy miles per hour De Havilland DH6's of 1918 have been replaced by supersonic Panavia Tornadoes which, though not based at West Freugh regularly use the airfield facilities. The duties to which they were allotted meant that DH6's were only to be seen around Luce Bay and the western coastline. Today with most Galloway airspace an authorised low flying area Tornadoes are frequently seen flying low and fast over all parts of the region.

In two peacetime decades between 1918 and 1938 RAF contact with Galloway was sustained by the flying boats which regularly visited Loch Ryan. Then on 1 January 1937 4 Armament Training School opened its doors at West Freugh heralding an era of increased activity when, following the outbreak of war in 1939, training facilities expanded as the western location was considered likely to be free from enemy interference.

Within two years five airfields or airstrips, a hospital, two air sea rescue units, two flying boat bases, a marine craft training school, an embarkation unit and several storage bases were in use or under construction.

Enemy aircraft were not to be unknown over Galloway. A press release issued by the Ministry of Information was published by the local press in August 1944. This showed that in ten incidents since the outbreak of war 26 enemy bombs or mines had been dropped in Galloway, thirteen in each of the two Counties. Virtually all had dropped in open country, no lives were lost and only minor

33. Wreckage of Heinkel He111 which crashed on Cairnsmore of Fleet, 9th August, 1940.

injuries caused. Probably the most serious incident occurred in May 1941 when eight bombs and one mine dropped, probably abandoned, on a farm a few miles from Port William. A farm cottage in which ten people were asleep suffered considerable blast damage, fortunately apart from shock the only injuries were slight caused by flying glass from shattered windows. A bomb which dropped on 20 October broke windows in Buittle Parish Church which stands in an isolated position between Castle Douglas and Dalbeattie. On 9 August 1940 a Heinkel He111 of 1 Kampf Gruppe 4 flying on a mine-laying mission from Soesterberg in Holland crashed on Cairnsmore of Fleet causing consternation amongst those of the populace whose philosophy had till then been "they will never reach here". Some time later on the night of 25 March 1943 a Dornier Do217E of 7 Kampf Gruppe 2, also based in Holland, fired a short machine gun burst at the airfield beacon of 10(0) AFU, Dumfries, without causing any damage, shortly before it crashed at 1250 feet on 1496 feet high Cairnharrow, four and half miles due west of Gatehouse of Fleet. Some eighteen months later when censorship permitted the *'Galloway News'* reported on 26 August 1944 that 'one crew member was killed in the crash, three others were taken into custody by the police soon after daylight'. The aircraft was loaded with 'thousands of incendiary bombs of which 700 exploded in the crash causing little damage.'

Lufftwaffe flights over Wigtownshire in 1940 and 1941 were not widely known until 1999 when the Royal Commission on the Ancient and Historical Monuments of Scotland published a catalogue listing 126 Luftwaffe photographs of sites in Scotland which the Commission had just received from the USA where they had been held since 1945. Four of these photographs depict RAF bases in Wigtownshire. Titles and dates are:

West Freugh Airfield	18 October 1940
Kidsdale Airfield	12 December 1940
Stranraer (Loch Ryan)	2 January 1941
Wigtown Airfield	2 January 1941

The photograph of Stranraer shows the greater part of Loch Ryan and indicates the location of Stranraer and Wig Bay flying boat bases as 'seaplane manoeuvering areas'. The photographs were taken in daylight hours and all have excellent definition. The Luftwaffe used a variety of Junkers and Dornier aircraft for long range photographic reconnaisance over Scotland usually flying at heights of around 30000 feet. The camera used was an Rb 30, weighing 160 lbs, two of which were mounted vertically in the bomb bay space, one large lensed target camera and one mapping camera with a small focal length.

Flying boat operations from Loch Ryan played an imortant part in the campaign to protect vital Atlantic sea lanes however, there can be no doubt that the greater contribution to the war effort from the RAF in Galloway came from the training units. It is not an exaggeration to say that thousands of Observers, Navigators, Bomb Aimers and Air Gunners on completion of training in Galloway passed to Operational Training Units and thence to the operational squadrons of Bomber Command. In addition to the many aircrews trained for them at Stranraer and Castle Kennedy, Coastal Command relied upon the school at Corsewall to supply trained crews for marine craft without which air sea rescue units and flying boat bases could not have operated. Further the maintenance unit at Wig Bay, one of the largest flying boat bases in the United Kingdom, played a major part in supplying and maintaining the flying boats used by Coastal and Transport Commands.

Over the years since 1918, particularly between 1939 and 1945, many thousands of airmen and airwomen of many nationalities have served in many capacities with the Royal Air Force in Galloway. Hopefully they retained happy memories of a sojourn in, using the local idiom, "Bonnie Gallowa'".

ACKNOWLEDGEMENTS

Crown Copyright material in the Public Office Record is reproduced
by permission of the Controller of Her Majesty's Stationary Office.
Document references are:

AIR 1:   215;216;236;237;238;324;328;329;640
AIR 10:   4039
AIR 14:   977;987
AIR 15:   67;325;466;467;735;1698
AIR 24:   569;570;1482;1513
AIR 27:   587;826;910;936;1108;1135;1208;1292;1293;
            1294;1347;1414;1415;1458;1625;1807;1921;
            2128;2176
AIR 28:   125;160;770;772;773;774;1293
AIR 29:   6;40;42;440;448;449;544;590;597;605;609;629
            702;764;978;1014;1063;1203;1466;1553;1554;
            1599;1834;1921;2108;2410
AVIA 15:   1698

For permission to reproduce photographs thanks are due to:-
        ROYAL AIR FORCE MUSEUM (RAFM)
        IMPERIAL WAR MUSEUM (IWM)
        PUBLIC RECORD OFFICE (PRO)
        WIGTOWN DISTRICT MUSEUM
        MRS T MILLAR, GLASSERTON
        MR D NELSON, STRANRAER
        MRS R REID, NEWTON STEWART

Ministry of Defence (MOD) whose Crown Copyright
photographs are reproduced with permission of the
Controller of Her Majesty's Stationary Office.

Assistance and advice has also been freely given by the
Curator and Staff of the Wigtown District Museum and the
Reference Librarian, Ewart Library, Dumfries.

Quotation from 'Ground Staff' by courtesy of the Society of
Authors